HERMETIC
FUNDAMENTALS
REVEALED

"Showing in perfect sequence the stages of
unfoldment through which the soul passes
to reach Illumination."

Dr. A. S. Raleigh

ISBN 1-56459-370-3

CONTENTS

LESSON I

THE PHYSICAL BODY

The physical body constitutes our vehicle of consciousness for the physical plane. Without such vehicle of consciousness it would be utterly impossible for mankind to come into cognition of anything connected with the physical plane, physical consciousness being solely through the physical vehicle.

By the physical body, we mean in this sense both the Gross Body and the Etheric Double or Magnetic Body.

It should be borne in mind, that physical matter, that is to say, all matter on the physical plane, operates on Seven Subplanes, the seven notes, so to speak, of the physical octave, all matter vibrating on the highest note, being etheric, the undifferentiated ether, the two lower notes representing the electrical and magnetic, the three constituting the triad, the tertiary, the positive and negative aspects of the electrical and magnetic principles constituting the quaternary of Earth, Air, Fire and Water, or Carbon, Nitrogen, Oxygen and Hydrogen, the four lower principles or notes.

It should be understood, however, that in the etheric, these are not the carbon, hydrogen, oxygen and nitrogen of physics, but are rather what we might term metaphysical, being in reality the odoriferous ether, the gustiferous ether, the luminiferous ether and the tangiferous ether, which descending to the physical plane, manifest themselves in the gases known to chemistry, by the combination of which, the eighty-six so-called elements in their Molecular Units are formed, the molecules being simply structures formed by the association of multitudes of atoms. Of these seven elemental ethers the higher form the Ether of sound, the highest Tattva on the physical plane being associated with the upper triad.

The Etheric Double, or Magnetic Body in man is formed of the Physical Energy of the upper triad, or the three higher notes and is, therefore, composed of ether, electricity and magnetism and is consequently a vehicle of consciousness for the three higher notes of the physical octave throughout the universe. In other words, the three higher sub-planes of the physical plane manifest themselves through the magnetic body, whereas the four lower manifest themselves through the gross physical body, it being only able to respond to and take notice of and transmit vibration emanating from the four lower sub-planes of the physical plane.

The gross body is, in reality the duplicate on a lower plane, of the magnetic body. It conforms in every respect to the image presented in the magnetic body, which, in a certain sense, acts as a pattern for the gross body. The magnetic body is in the same form as the gross body; in fact, it would be more accurate to say the Gross Body is in the same form as the Magnetic Body, being its expression in a more dense and gross form, made of more dense and more gross substances, its fineness depending upon the material out of which it is composed and upon its vibratory susceptibility. Likewise the fineness of the Magnetic Body depends upon its ethers and their rate of vibration.

It should be borne in mind that the mission, so to speak, of the gross body, is to transmit to the consciousness, vibrations from the four lower sub-planes of the Physical Plane, and thus bring the Ego into conscious recognition of the things operating upon the four lower notes of the Physical Octave; it has no other purpose; therefore, the entire utility of all of its parts is in relation to this function.

In other words, the Gross Body is the organ whose function it is to transmit sensations relative to the four lower notes of the Physical Octave and to enable the Ego to act upon those four notes of the Physical Octave, the sensory and motor nerves being the live wires which enable this activity to take place. The sensory nerves are the wires which communicate the sensation resulting from vibration on those four notes to the consciousness. The motor nerves communicate the nervous stimuli sent forth at the mandate of the consciousness to the muscles, in order that they may perform those duties growing out of the condition brought about by those sensations. The muscular structure is specifically adapted to work of this kind. If you examine a muscle you will find it to be, in reality, a bundle of minute fibres, which are so fine that you can scarcely see them, the fibres laid in layers and then one layer upon another, until the bundle is formed; but if you will take the smallest muscular fibre and examine it carefully, you will see that it is, itself, a bundle of still smaller microscopic fibres. These minute fibres combine and form ropes, which, in turn, stack, so to speak, and form larger bundles, which are to combine to construct the muscle. The result will be that in a single muscle there will be, perhaps, millions of the smaller muscular fibres.

Now, these muscles are divided into two classes, voluntary and involuntary, an involuntary muscle being one whose movement is not under the control of our objective consciousness, not guided by the will; that is to say, the conscious will, while a voluntary muscle is. Now, the difference in their structure is this: in the involuntary muscles, the fibres go in only one direction, all lying straight, while in the voluntary muscles, they cross, making two directions of movement. Now, when there is a certain impulse transmitted to the muscle, it contracts; that is to say the fibres shorten. On the other hand, when the other impulse is transmitted, they relax or lengthen. Take the arm, for instance; you want to raise anything, and what is the result? The purpose to raise it, transmits a flow of energy, which causes the muscle running from the shoulder blade down the arm, to contract and shorten. The result is, the arm can no longer remain straight. It is drawn up and this pull, so to speak, resulting from the shortening of the muscular fibres, raises the weight which is held in the hand. Then when the muscle relaxes, the arm straightens, we let it down.

We undertake to take a step. A flow of energy is transmitted to the muscle of the leg, which causes it to shorten and thus flex the leg. When we let it down again the muscle is relaxed and the leg straightens, and so through the entire system. We are contracting and relaxing the muscles, that is, shortening and lengthening them and thus all those motions are taking place.

A voluntary muscle, because of the fact that the fibres cross, are laid in cross sections, is capable of relaxing and contracting in two different directions, making, therefore, two movements, backward and forward, instead of one, making a square instead of a line in its operations.

There are some muscles observed to be partially crossed, showing a few cross sections. This has been noticed in recent years much more than formerly and, therefore, indicates that, by reason of man's development, he is acquiring voluntary control of muscles which were formerly involuntary; but it should be borne in mind that the function of the muscles is to enable the body to move in accordance with the promptings of the consciousness as it is moved by the energy flowing to it, the function of the motor nerves being to transmit that energy to the muscle, making it move accordingly. The muscles move the bones, being attached at the ends to the bone, but not attached all the way along, being thus attached in such a way as to bend the bones at the joints, the bones acting as levers while the muscles act as the belts or cables which move them. The body is thus, through this activity of the muscles, made to move according to the promptings coming from the consciousness, and those promptings are in response to sensations which are received through the sensory nerves from the realm without.

It is also the function of the body, through the digestive apparatus and the organs of assimilation, etc., the microscopic cells, to take physical matter, in the form of food, into the system, dissolve it into its chemical constituents, finally reducing it to the finer electric, magnetic and etheric principles and then again bringing it into its own constituent elements, thus that it may be reproduced and perpetuated.

It is likewise, through its organs of elimination, the waste material, the worn out tissue, the scraps, so to speak, the rubbish, is eliminated and the effectiveness and efficiency of the body for the performance of its diverse functions maintained, for this depends largely upon the degree in which this nutrition and elimination are accomplished.

Were we deprived of a gross physical body, it would be utterly impossible to derive the slightest sensation from gross physical matter. It is, therefore, evident that man was intended to possess a gross body in order that he might maintain his relationship to the four lower notes of the physical octave and might be conscious of those things. In this way we can see the fallacy of the spiritualistic practice of invoking discarnate human spirits to tell them about physical matters. A discarnate spirit, having no gross body and having no subliminal counterpart of the gross body, as have the angels and God, beings who have always been spirits and not intended to have physical bodies—has, consequently, no way of coming into touch with the gross physical plane and can know absolutely nothing about it excepting what he has learned while he possessed a gross body. When the etheric double is lost, which, of course, takes place at the same time that the gross body is lost, he can know absolutely nothing of the three higher notes of the physical octave, because that is the function of the etheric double or magnetic body.

Not only does the Gross Body possess the organs necessary to its own activities, but it also possesses organs through which the higher principles function and it is necessary that this be true in order that those same higher principles may operate in conjunction with the gross body and express themselves in our physical consciousness. For this reason we have a number of organs which the doctors, in their infinite wisdom, have decided are entirely superannuated. They must have been there while we were monkeys or lizards or Betsy-bugs or something of the kind when we had need for them; they had some functional use, they occupied a physiological relation, but now they are entirely superannuated. One of these superannuated organs is the spleen. It is true, the learned gentlemen, once in a while, will consent that it must be associated with the production of white blood corpuscles or something of that kind, but they do not really know just what it is, and, in fact, it is so thoroughly superannuated that the best thing to do is to amputate it in cases of certain derangements; if it gets enlarged, just cut it out. Nevertheless, the fact remains that no man is ever himself after having his spleen removed, the amputation of a spleen inevitably leading to a condition of disorder which nothing can cure. The facts in the case are, the spleen is the physical organ of the Magnetic Body; has the same relation to that, that the heart has to the circulation of the blood, and through this organ the Magnetic Body travels and circulates, the etheric substance flowing in its circuits and passing through this organ, and thus the connection between the Etheric Body and the Gross Body is maintained. Whenever this organ is removed the Etheric Double is deprived of its organ, consequently the connection between it and the Gross Body is interfered with, is, to a certain extent broken up, and those disturbances which result from breaking up the affinity with the Magnetic Body and the Gross Physical Body, naturally result.

The Solar Plexus is the center through which Prana, the Life force circulates. It is also the physical storehouse for the Prana, which storehouse may be tapped in case of emergency.

The heart is not only the organ for the circulation of the blood, but is also the physical organ for the Desire Body, the emotional principles, and it is for this reason that emotional states have such a profound influence upon the circulation of the blood and the heart action.

The brain is, of course, the center of the circulation of the Mental Body, likewise, also, the Causal Body, the upper brain being the center of the causal body, the lower brain that of the mental body.

Another one of the organs which the scientists, in their wisdom, have decided is superannuated, is the Pineal Gland, in fact, some contend that while we were lizards, that was the eye, situated in the top of the head, but, through millions of transformations in our species, we finally developed a brain which grew up over and covered up that eye, and at last it became imbedded there and was atrophied. The Pineal Gland is, in reality the Center of the Buddhic Body or Soul. It is through this Body that the circulation takes place. It is an eye in the sense that it is the eye of seership. It is not the third eye of a lizard, but of a type of humanity much more perfect than we are at the present time. It is now being revived and will ultimately develop to its true proportions in the Buddhic race. True, it is atrophied, for most people's souls are decidedly atrophied, particularly those, very largely, of doctors of medicine and of surgeons.

The Spirit centers in an organ back of the forehead about an inch, between the eyes, and about an inch back, close to the pituitary body, this organ called by the Rosicrucians the "Silent Watcher," being the seat of the spirit.

It will, therefore, be seen that the Gross Physical Body is the vehicle on the four lower notes of the Physical Octave, for the manifestation of all the higher principles. It is also the central base for the Aura, that solid structure through which the Aura manifests itself.

The brain is developed in such a way as to perfectly adapt itself as the central organ of the Mental and Causal Bodies, the brain fibre and cells, convolutions and everything being formed in such a way as to most perfectly enable the manifestation of thought, each faculty of the mind having developed a specific organ of the brain as its functioning medium; likewise each thought has a particular combination of brain cells adapted to itself and it is utterly impossible for a thought to come into manifestation without first having developed a brain cellular combination adapted to its manifestation.

The entire Gross Body is, therefore, seen to be in perfect adaptation to the manifestation of the higher principles; it is, in fact, their product and they can manifest on the physical plane only as this physical vehicle is adapted to such manifestation. Not only is this true, but in exact proportion as the finer principles develop, become finer, more subtile, reach a higher degree of perfection, in like manner does the Gross Body respond. Evolution of the Gross Physical Body, is seen to follow directly that of the higher principles. The body thus responds to all those higher activities and, consequently, we can tell the temperament of a person by the formation of his body.

The Brain is not only the seat of the Mental Body, but it is the central base, as it were, of the Gross Body. There is not an organ nor a muscle in the entire body, there is not a bone, there is not a cell in the entire gross body but what is the negative pole of a corresponding cell or organ in the brain and the stimulational development of that brain center will have the reflex action of developing, stimulating and governing its physical pole. Likewise, exercise of a muscle of a part of the body will call out, stimulate and develop the corresponding part of the brain. There is thus this inter-relation between the brain and the balance of the body which is so thoroughly brought out in Psychic Physiological Science.

It is for this reason that mental temperaments are always accompanied by corresponding physical temperamental states and conditions. Every part of the body, the formation of the finger and thumb nail, every turn of the body, every line of the hand, even the very formation of the graining of the skin, the lines and everything indicating conditions of the brain, which, in turn, are but the expressions of the conditions of the higher principles, and those principles, in turn, are influenced by the condition of the Gross Body. The food we eat and everything of that kind have their influence upon the formation of the higher principles as well as influencing the bodily condition.

The Etheric Double is never separated from the Gross Body for any length of time to speak of. It always maintains its connection and is the plastic medium though which the Desire body and all the higher principles are connected with the Gross Body. The Etheric Double is indicated by the color pink or more accurately speaking, the color of a fresh blown peach blossom, which is its color when pure and uncontaminated. It may be of different shades and tints, but this is the proper color, and any deviation from this will indicate a degree of corruption according to the shade or tint which is predominant, and wherever we go we carry with us this tint or some variation of it, and any pink that may be seen in the Aura will indicate the presence of the Magnetic Body.

It should be understood that the magnetic forces operating through the magnetic body are physical. It is physical electro-magnetic force, the electricity being the positive, masculine principle and the magnetism the negative, feminine, but it is physical, being the same kind of electricity which is generated in the battery and the same kind of magnetism which is found in the magnet—not vital, but physical.

This is the function of the Physical Vehicle, both the

Gross Body and the Magnetic Body, namely, to enable the ego to maintain his connection, his relationship with and to the physical plane, to correlate himself and to come into conscious recognition of the vibrations of the Physical Octave through physical sensations.

LESSON II

THE ASTRAL BODY

The Astral Body is the vehicle of the emotions and de-sires. All energy vibrating upon the astral octave is astral matter. or desire stuff. When we feel an emotion there is imparted to the astral matter a vibration corresponding to that particular emotion. And, also, the emotional vibrations group themselves upon the different vibratory notes of the astral body according to the class to which they belong. That is to say, that emotion classifies itself, it has the divisions to which it properly revolves. Now, when we realize that emotion is susceptible of classification and is capable of division into various classes, we have first the positive, and second, the negative emotion; that is to say, the positive are those emotions that cause the whirl in the vibration to lead outward so as to produce something; in a sense vibrations that lead into the emotional depths in the inside body outward to its surface, thus outward and positive. Then, again, there is the negative, because of its drawing inward the inward trend which is coming about all the time as the effect of something, the vortex which draws everything inward. Thus, we see the difference between the two classes of emotions, and everyone who has ever had any experience in healing or anything of that kind, knows the fact that the negative emotions are very often quite troublesome. A person governed by those negative emotions is likely not only to take on disease but any other disease that they come in contact with, good, bad or indifferent.

The negative state of the emotions produce in the astral body a number of tracks, which invite, which draw in all the emotional states which may be in operation throughout the astral plane, as it is said in the Bible "The thing I greatly fear has come upon me". This expectation that something is coming thus makes the Astral body negative and draws in those very forces which it ordinarily would throw off, as it were, or those very forces, we mean, would bring on an inward motion and bring on this condition.

Now, when the astral body is positive, the whirl is expressing itself through those forces that whirl outward, and thus the astral is acting upon the external.

Now, remember that astral body is the microcosm, the exact duplicate of the astral world. This astral world being the whole desire force, the realm of desire throughout the universe. Now, the astral body of man is the microcosm of the astral world, being polarized with it. If it is positive it is producing effects on the astral plane; if it is negative it is being influenced by the astral plane.

It is not necessary that we should be positive all the time. If the whirl is positive and is always dominating, you will never get anything except what you originate yourself; and there is no use of making fools of ourselves. Negative states are just as necessary as the positive. Negativity is a state of positive absolute demand. While the positive state is a state of outward activity, therefore we have got to maintain that attitude of asking if we get anything. Remember, that the difference between the positive and negative emotion is that the negative is bringing it within and the positive is bringing out that which is within and acting upon the external, and there are certain emotions which have one or the other of those effects, for instance, courage, ambition, resolution, hope, optimism, etc., generally is a thought or feeling of independence and everything of that kind are positive. The negative emotion, such as fear, uneasiness, horror, remorse, pain or penitence, doubt, lack of faith, reverence, veneration, prayer, all those states are negative states; and you will notice that some of the highest emotions were negative just as some of the lower emotions are positive, and all pessimistic emotion is negative, except in those conditions where your optimism is for somebody who is doing something for you, expecting something from the external. Thus we have this state of being which is continually expressing itself in those respects. Now the Astral vehicle is buoyed up with those various states of vibration, and every emotion has its particular vibration. When we have those various emotional states we have to depend upon them, we have to recognize the fact that they will carry on their rates of vibration, will carry on their work.

No two emotions, no matter how much alike they may be are specifically of the same rate of vibration. Thus they form different influences, different sounds, and those rates of vibration produce different geometrical figures in the astral matter. The more material these emotions are, the nearer the physical they are, the more black they become, so if you are able to see an astral body, clairvoyantly, you will notice that there is a good deal of dirty color there; you will recognize the earthy character of the vibrations; on the other hand, you will see perhaps that the vibrations are clear and colors bright, which will indicate the highest colors that pertain to that particular vehicle of prana, or life force. For this reason you will never see the nature of the astral body without the life principle prana, flowing through it

—and prana is rose-colored. If you see in the astral body that tint, the rose color, it indicates a greater degree of vitality, the more prana the more vitality.

Now, also, while it is true that this body is blue, yet the positive force, the electrical, or masculine, which is red, on whatever plane the masculine force is found, will, of course, be active to a greater or less extent. Therefore, the more red that you see in the astral body, the more positive force, the more of the electrical, and the masculinity is being expressed through that vehicle; and for that reason, we have the greatest degree of masculinity according as we have the red color. If the blue color predominates it is more feminine.

If you see the purple, which is blue and red, it is more of the positive aspect of emotion. Purple, therefore, will indicate the emotion, the positivity being expressed, the color of occultism, of mastership, so to speak, because it is the master force, the will united with the emotion. Suppose you see lavender in the color—that is more spiritual; the emotion approaching more to the spiritual; the lighter the tint the more spiritual it becomes.

Violet is a very high rate of vibration; it is astral activity on a very intense plane. It is very near the color of masculinity. Indigo is the color of magic; the paler indigo is the more indicative of the occult power.

Now, you come to a pale azure blue. The azure is both blue and green, in a sense united. Green is the color of action; it is also the color of nature; it is one aspect of the feminine color, more intensely feminine than the ordinary blue; it is the color that the Druids wore, the emerald green. This together with green is the astral color. If it approaches the white of the spirit, it indicates that the astral is drawing near to the spirit, and it is coming near the astral. These are the indications that those colors will show.

Now, whatever colors you see, you will understand, are mean, that is, they indicate the emotions that express themselves at that time. You cannot look at it at any moment and tell their color exactly, because it expresses the emotion at that particular instant. Examining at different times the mean of those colors you will be able to estimate the mean of those vibrations. When you have ascertained the cause of those states of activity, and also, the general character of the being, you will be able to estimate the value of the colors at any given time.

The astral vehicle is what is called in the Bible "The Heart." It is also kama rupa, the body of desire of the Hindus. It is the vehicle through which all the desires function. All the emotions express themselves through this astral vehicle. Now, the heart is not only the channel of the circulation of the blood, but the astral body really circulates through it. Owing to the fact that astral vehicle circulates through the heart is due the terrible action of emotion on the heart. The astral body is the vehicle of the prana; the prana does not act upon the heart as its channel, but circulates through the Solar Plexus. It is, also, the great store-house of prana; prana is stored up there and circulates, acting in and out through the solar plexus and thus through the astral body. When we understand this we can see the reason why troubles of the solar plexus will have such a terribly injurious effect on the vitality.

Now, while this is true, there is something more which is true in regard to the astral body. Now, the astral is capable of separation from the body, the being clothed in the astral can leave the gross physical body behind, leaving the physical body for days at a time, the body remaining in a state of trance. The long trance is simply a case of where the being is out on the astral plane. The astral is really out. A number of our dreams are nothing in the world but our memories of experiences, that we have had on a higher plane of nature, generally the astral plane. We go and see things and they are expressed on our astral consciousness, and we forget them. We are not able to impress them on our brain with sufficient exactness to take notice of them. They are not what we ordinarily look for; very often we see people we have never seen before. You will go to a place and it may seem perfectly familiar to you, yet you may never have gone there in the physical body, and you may know all about it. In such a case the people have really been there, they have really gone there and had those experiences. And going to those places in the physical body they remembered what they had seen before, just as when they experience those haunting memories, of something that they have seen in the past, and the struggle of a past memory is simply the effort to bring your superconscious experiences down into your conscious activities. The nightmare frightens people. They have the nightmare; they are really in the astral life. They see those things and go through experiences and when the time comes they can not understand it, they think of something terrible. They think it merely visionary, when really they are actual experiences that they have had on that plane; but they find it difficult to recall the experiences they had when they return to consciousness. But it is possible to do it.

There is an army of invisible helpers who are employed on the astral plane to help and assist all those who are in need of help; they have their physical bodies and go out in their astrals for the express purpose of working. There is still an army of invisible teachers. They are carrying on their work on the astral plane at night while the physical is asleep. There are conventions where a lot of astrals are present, taking in the deliberations, and telepathically participating in the deliberations, contributing their part to the instruction of the body. In fact if we could only realize it, the life on the astral plane is something of the very same kind as the life going on the physical plane. It is the life of Desire, while this is a life of action, physical action, which is as the reflection here on the physical plane of the activities of the Desire World. The astral body is the vehicle in which we can function more easily and perfectly on that plane and be perfectly intelligent. One is just about as complete as the other.

LESSON III

THE MENTAL BODY

In the first place, you must be able to conceive of mind being separated and apart from thoughts. The great trouble in all investigations along this line is that people confuse mind and thought. You must conceive mind as existing before any thinking took place. This may sound very coarse and gross to some of you; you have been taught that mind is the highest activity of the soul. It is material, nevertheless, which I will endeavor to show you before we get through. Mind is the highest aspect of thought, and when you understand this you are then able to understand the relation of all those things. Now, this may sound to you at first to be not very definite, but as a matter of fact there is nothing any more far-reaching than this statement.

Mind is the material of which thought is made. Mind is one of the planes of nature. If there were not a man in the world there would still be mind; if there were nothing created, no object created, yet there still would be mind. Mind is the mental substance, that force which exists in the world without. It is one of the aspects of the world.

We have five octaves of vibration in Nature, namely, the Spiritual, the Buddhic, the Mental, the Astral, and the Physical. First, there is the physical octave, covering the vibrations which manifest as the undifferentiated Ether, in its positive and negative differentiations of electricity and magnetism, together with the earth, air, fire and water, or in modern technical terminology, carbon, nitrogen, oxygen and hydrogen, positive and negative activities of these two principles.

(23)

Then, there is, second, the astral octave, which includes also life, which we learned about in the last lesson; and there is the mental octave, and there are two octaves above the mental plane.

The Mental Octave includes seven notes of vibration. The four lower notes of this octave are devoted to the region of concrete thought, the three higher notes are in the region of abstract thought, making the Septenary of the Mental Octave. This must sound like attenuated moonshine, and yet it is exact science.

You will find that there is a perfect harmony and perfect relation working all the way through. Now, mind movements express themselves in atoms, that is, ultimate atoms, electrons and molecules that are gathered together by reason of a harmonious rate of vibration expressed in rhythm; and simple thought is an organism formed by a movement of the atoms of mind; that is, mental atoms being drawn together by a common rate of vibration, they are held together and thus form an organism. A compound thought is a number of these thoughts, which are drawn together and held in position by a common chord and form a compound organism; a complex thought is a number of these compound thoughts drawn together and are dominated by a common tone, thereby being held together so as to form a complex thought structure; a thought form is a mass of mental matter ensouled by complex thoughts; which is being taught in our lessons on Motion and Number. That is, in the lesson on the Rhythm of Mind, which is the seventh lesson. These matters are made plainer in some respects there than at present we have time for.

The thing I must impress upon your intelligence is that mind is force, separate and apart from thought; thought is an organism which is developed as a result of this mental activity. Now, remember, therefore, that mind exists separate and apart from thought, and it may astonish you when we enunciate this so often, but this is something that scientists, psychologists, in the past have denied. The fundamental principle of the schools in the past was to deny that thought was a thing, to deny that it had any existence; only that it was a kind of condition, not a thing. Thought has a tangible existence; it is a material substance. Rather, mind, of which thought is composed, is a material substance. Now, the brain has been developed for the express purpose of expressing thought; in other words, mental matter acts through the tissue of the brain, and it is so developed as to offer the requisite degree of resistance to enable mind to express itself in thought. The different classes of vibration must have groups of mental matter, fibre and cells adapted to respond to that particular rhythm into combination of vibration, and as the class to which a thought belongs always coincides with the class of vibration to which it belongs, thus rates of vibration express themselves in thoughts; in other words, that organism will express itself in the faculty pertaining to it.

Not only is this true, but each cell is developed and has a certain vibratory relation and vibratory capacity, which will express itself in that way, and the various brain fibres are trained and have that relation, that vibratory capacity, so that they will respond to that rate of vibration, and thus express themselves in that thought. The brain is merely the organism established by nature for the purpose of expressing itself in vibratory activity. Remember that it is but the physical organism for the activity of the mind. Now, as the mind expresses itself through that organism, that being its center of activity, and expressing itself through that; in other words, thought coming into manifestation according as it brings itself into that vibratory expression, what is the inevitable result? Simply this: that thought is an organism, a being, a body, when it is expressing itself in this way. It should be borne in mind, that as mind, expressing itself through thought, is being generated, it flows outward from its center, forming a kind of sphere, in one sense of the word, which it will express or manifest, when it thus forms a body (and this is the origin of the expression "Mental Body"). In this way we get the idea of mind expressing itself as a body, as another principle in the human constitution.

It is only when we realize this, that mind exists as a body, as another principle in the human constitution and not merely as a kind of visionary something we don't know what, (the way the most of the physicists would have us to believe); it is in this way that we can see real truth.

Now, the mind force forms a body, which entirely permeates the astral body and goes on down to the etheric double, and in the course of time to the physical body. There is nowhere where mind is not present. Remember that mind is the principle of Man, where it transcends the astral principle and rises above to the soul, or Buddhi, and expresses itself through the brain. What then are we to understand in relation to the mind? You know it has been the theory for a very long time among psychologists and mental physiologists, that mind was related to the genus Homo, and they supposed that nobody but Man was in possession of Mind. This is not true, for mind is a principle of Nature, and extends to the Animal, Vegetable, and even to the Mineral kingdoms; Man's mind being different only in degree to all the other beings in this respect.

Schopenhauer makes this very clear, and shows, that in nature, Will is manifested among animals and also among plants. The bean vine illustration, in which he shows the Will in Nature, covers this illustration of Will in the Vegetable kingdom. The radical of a bean, in its efforts to reach the surface of the earth, came in contact with a shoe sole, and it couldn't get through; there were forty thread holes. It divided itself into forty filaments and passed through the thread holes, and then united again, and went to the surface, and made a stalk of beans. It was only when digging in the ground, that they discovered how the plant had figured it all out and had decided just what had to take place. This is not instinct; instinct does not stimulate any such intelligence as that. Any plant will seek the light no matter where it is; not only is that true, but climbing plants will go through crevices, go over walls and hunt for a place, where they can attach themselves. They really hunt for those places. Therefore, we find in the plant world abundant evidence of intelligence, not instinct. Not only is this true, but Darwin's work on Vegetable Mold, shows, that earth worms have the capacity to learn by experience. If they do learn, they must have the reasoning faculties. You may go wherever you please; you will find that plants and animals have reasoning faculties. It naturally follows, that those states of existence have Mind just as much in the absolute as Man has, though least in degree; that is the only difference—least in degree. Now, the Mind is not purely a human activity, a human achievement, but is something which is universally applicable throughout nature. All forms of life, or forms of existence are in possession of this power, namely Mind. It is manifesting itself through all the activities of life. Now, as a matter of fact, Mind expresses itself through this

Mental body (The mental body is the form which mind takes in its activities) permeating the astral body.

As we said before, the highest three notes of the mental octave express themselves in abstract thought. Now, what is the result? There are two distinct bodies formed. One is formed by concrete thought and is formed out of the four lower notes of the mental octave: the other is formed out of abstract thought and is the result of activities of abstract thinking; and represents the triad, the three higher notes of the mental octave. This is ordinarily called "the causal body." All the concrete activities are the result of abstract mental activity; all these abstract mental activities act through the causal body. Now, when you stop to think, it is a fact that only a small per cent of the human race think in the abstract, and you may readily see the causal body is relatively weak in comparison to the mental body. When a man dies, his astral body leaves the physical behind, and goes out into the astral plane, and in time his mental body goes out into the mental plane abandoning the astral, and in time his causal body leaves the mental body. It is generally claimed by Theosophy, that it is a fact that the soul ultimately leaves the causal body.

There is no evidence of immortality offered by any kind of Spiritual phenomena. There is one death on the astral plane and two deaths on the mental plane. After the physical death, there is no evidence of perpetuity of existence; therefore, it does not prove these things. We mean both the lower mental body and, also, the causal body in contra-distinction from the physical and astral.

Now all concrete thought goes to build up this concrete vehicle, the mental body; all abstract thought builds up the abstract vehicle, the causal body. Whenever we are thinking along those lines we are exercising an influence along that direction; wherever we turn we are doing that kind of work.

The Mental Body is yellow; the Causal Body approaches the gold in its color, just as the Astral Body is some shade of blue. The Etheric Double is pink, or rather the color of fresh blown peach blossoms. Red is positive or masculine; blue on the astral plane indicates the feminine; the red indicates a preponderance of masculinity no matter where it may be. Now, on through each of the bodies there is a certain state of consciousness corresponding to the particular principle involved. The mental consciousness is primarily the super-consciousness. It is possible to leave the astral body behind entirely in addition to the physical and go out in the mental body to travel on the mental plane. The astral activity is not the only one which transcends the physical, for it is possible for us to rise above the astral into the mental and carry on those activities; no question about it, it is possible to do it. We have done it ourselves. The mental body is the highest aspect of what might properly be termed Mind. The soul and the spirit are the two forces above the mental body. The mental body functions the various centers, and has as its center the brain, just as the astral body, the heart; the prana, the solar plexus and the etheric body the spleen.

You may see the mental body projected; both may be projected as the case may be. The color of the causal body may be some shade of gold, while the color of the mental body will be some shade of yellow, but not golden.

As the various thoughts cannot express themselves until they meet resistance through the tissue, the tissue must offer resistance in order that they may express themselves; all manifestations are due to resistance. Now, suppose there is no brain fibre and no brain cells which have the same key-notes which the thought has; they will not resist it, but it will go right through them, and no resistance will be offered. There is a continual tendency to alter the tissue in accordance with the vibration which has to pass through it, so that in time that tissue is so modified that it will resist, it will acquire that rate of vibration, and so will resist that vibration of the mind and the result is, there will be a new brain fibre, and new brain cells develop, or else the brain cells will be modified so that they will respond to that activity, and then that thought will be able to manifest itself.

You understand that the mental process is the process of the "ever-becoming;" it is not stationary in any sense whatever, but is going through a continual process of evolution, and this is the process of the "Ever-becoming," So as the cells strive to adapt themselves to new conditions, they will assume new vibratory relations, vibratory capacities; and assuming these, they will express themselves in certain ways. Now, it is true those capacities, those vibratory activities, expressing themselves in those different ways, constitute the true foundations upon which our mental progress really depends. All the way through it is a progress of the "ever-becoming" and those vibratory expressions organize brain fibres and brain cells to properly express themselves; that is really the truth. It is a new organism of tissue which is adapted to the expression of that impulse. And bear in mind, this complex brain structure is merely the instrument which the mind is employing to enable it to manifest itself in thought; it being the physical organ of the mental body.

LESSON IV

THE AURA

"Aura" is from a Sanskrit word, which means literally "that which flows." It is something flowing out from a common center. Now, the aura in regard to man is really the etheric double, the astral body, together with the life-force, prana, and the mental body—and by the mental body, we include the causal body, the mental body in Theosophical literature used in reference to the lower manas; that part which is made up of the four lower notes, or sub-planes of the mental plane. The causal occupies the three higher notes of the mental octave; but in our usage of the term, we include the causal as the part of the mental body. The aura includes all that we have gone over. But that is not all. The aura also includes the soul, and the spirit, the Buddhi and the Atma. The six principles of man, excepting the gross physical body are included in the aura. It is the combination of the six principles which constitutes the aura. If we are to understand what this is, we must begin with, the etheric double, or magnetic body, which permeates every cell and tissue of the gross body and extends beyond it. We have, entirely permeating this magnetic body, the astral, or desire body, which passes through and permeates this and extends outward. There is, at the same time, permeating the astral body, the prana, or life force. Then, we have the mental body, which permeates this, and then, in turn, the causal body permeating the mental body, although ordinarily, we use these two together. The Buddhic permeates the causal body, and then the spirit, or

(31)

Atma, permeates the Buddhic body whenever it can.

Do not get the idea, that so many people have of stratifications. The idea that some of the epicureans used to have in Greece, that the different principles are in layers, one outside of another, (something like onion skins) is entirely erroneous. To illustrate, let us suppose that we have a box filled with marbles. The marbles will represent the gross body. There will be quite a number of cavities between them. In the same way, we now put in a lot of shot, and let that run in between the marbles. This shot will represent the astral body. Then we fill our box with water, letting the sand absorb the water. The water will represent the life principle. In this water there is air. The air, now, which is permeating the water, will represent the mental body. The oxygen in the air, which is permeating that; let it represent the causal body. Now, permeating this oxygen is the prana. The recognition of this fact, that the prana is separate from the oxygen, allows us to represent the Buddhic body. Now, the spirit will be represented by something as permeating the prana. This goes beyond the ordinary comprehension, so the illustration cannot be used any further here. But bear in mind, that one principle is permeating the other. It is not a lot of shells, one outside of the other.

The finer substances penetrate the grosser. Let us see what this implies: Remember, that the various principles have their different colors. And if you look at an aura and see it in its completeness, you will see the aura —you cannot see into the body—surrounding the body by an outflowing substance, a kind of aura flowing out which will be pink, or the color of a fresh-blown peach blossom. It will be sufficiently near that color for you to recognize it. This is the magnetic body, the etheric double. Then, you will see permeating this, flowing outward, a kind of aureal, so to speak, which is of the color of some shade of blue—it may be of different shades. If it is of any shade of blue, it is the astral body. At the same time permeating this, you will see a radiance of rose color flowing out and through all this, flowing all the while through it. This is the life principle, Prana. Permeating this astral you will also see a yellow glory, so to speak, which will represent the mental body. No matter what shade of yellow, so long as it does not approach orange. Then you will see an orange light, which is shining through and flowing out through the yellow; this is the Soul, or Buddhi; if you look still deeper, you will find shining out through all this a white radiance, the Atma, or the human spirit.

There will, also be seen a number of modifications of these fundamental colors, according to the perfection of the Aura. These are the colors, which the bodies assume, at least they will assume some modification of these colors, and when those colors have been assumed, then we will see the quality, the value of the aura.

If a person, or a patient, is sick, if he is diseased, morally or physically, you will see that the aura has a certain amount of dirt, so to speak, (that is the nearest way we can express it, the sensation which you will get) there will be a dirty appearance present in the aura. It will present the conception, or appearance, of being soiled, and whatever amount of dirt there may be in the aura it will be here indicated; either moral or physical pollutions. The clearer the color, the freer from contaminations. Clearness in a certain principle indicates its freedom from all contaminating influences. Then, brilliancy, the brightness which it assumes, indicates its degree of perfection along its own particular line.

Now, all these together form the aura—the outflowing,

which is flowing out from the center. Remember, the aura
is generated within those principles, and represents those
principles as flowing out. We ordinarily speak of them
as being beyond the gross body. As a matter of fact,
it permeates the entire body in our ordinary consciousness; we mean that body which extends beyond the gross
physical body.

The aura is egg-shape, usually extending from the top
of the head downward to the feet. The gross body is in
the center of the aura, standing in that position. The aura
extends on an average, from about two inches to two feet
around in every direction from the gross body; although
in the case of a Mahatma, the causal itself is about the
size of an ordinary two-storied house; and in the case of
a Buddhi, his aura extends for about two miles in every
direction, and he is perfectly conscious of what is going
on in that radius of space; different people, however,
have it representing different states of being. Towards
sunset, you can let a person stand at a distance from you
and you will be able to see the aura, which he gives; you
can see the etheric double radiating from the body; but
for most people this is impossible. Then there are some
people whose sight is so acute, that they can see in an
aura a number of different bodies.

Now, do not get the idea, that the aura is confined to
the human being. There is no greater error than assuming that the aura is peculiarly human, a human acquire-
ment. The aura is found in animals just as much as it is
in man, though they are not so perfectly developed. It is
also found to vary according to the degree of perfection
of the animal, and it is found that the principle is precisely the same as it is in man—the only difference between the aura of an animal and that of a man, being
only in degree, not a difference in kind. This proves con-

clusively to the Occultist that the animal has the same seven principles just as man has. Man is in no way superior to the animal except in degree; the septenary principle is the same. For this fact, we are able to see animals clairvoyantly. The aural communication not only passes from man to animal, but from animal to man.

We used to have a friend in Arkansas, who raised numbers of sheep to sell and to kill for meat, etc. He told us on a number of occasions he had gone to the pen, and had made up his mind to kill a certain sheep; and immediately without the making of a motion, the very moment he had made up his mind in regard to the particular sheep he was to kill, that one would begin to make frantic efforts to get away. There was no trouble to find the others. But if we assume that the telepathic communication of man's thought goes to the consciousness of the animal, then we can understand these things; but not otherwise. Now, there is another peculiar thing; a wild animal is not afraid of a person who never kills animals; a vegetarian can get a great deal closer to a wild animal than a person who believes in eating the meat of animals. If you go into the matter thoroughly and clearly, you will come to the realization of the fact that the animals have the capacity for acquiring a knowledge of the intentions of the person toward them. Now in India, Yogis will go out into the Jungle and lie down and go to sleep, and while they are asleep the tigers will come and lick their bare feet. Anybody else would not dare to go there without an eight-bore rifle and two or three native attendants. They have nothing but love, and never eat meat, never take the life of an animal, and the tigers recognize them by their aura. They sense those conditions, that state of their being.

But it is not simply that animals possess auras, but

plants likewise. We have gone through an orchard and we
can literally taste the peaches and apples growing on the
trees. This is a statement of facts. We can stand ten feet
from the trees and taste the fruit, and not even know how
it tastes. Now, the only possible explanation for that, is
that the aura of that fruit is radiating out and filling the
air. Not only is that true, but you can put a plant or fruit
in the room, set it down on the table and without touching
the fruit at all, without knowing what kind it is, we can
tell whether it is sweet or sour. We have seen women
paring apples and have made the remark, without having
tasted them at all, "My, how sour those apples are."
That is clairgustea, in a sense, in some state of development. There must be a law underlying it. We see that
every bit of fruit has its aura, not only a tree, but the
fruit also. The odor of flowers shows that they have an
aura; what you sense is the etheric double of that flower,
its etheric principle. It proves the aura of the flower.
But, this is not all.

Not only do flowers, plants, etc., have auras, but also
minerals possess it. We know a lady down in Arkansas,
who can take a piece of ore in her hand and by the taste,
which she gets in her mouth, she will be able to tell you
what it is—she assays it by the taste. Now, this proves in
itself, that they have auras, else it would not be possible
to tell them in that way. The sea stones, the looking into
stones, the gazing into crystals, would only be possible
upon the assumption, that they have auras, that they are
souls, because their auras, their influence will establish
there and become conscious of those things. But that is
not all the evidence, that we have to offer. We have sat by
the roadside, and watched the auric vibrations of rocks.
We have watched them and seen the different colors
emanating from them; we know that flint and rocks, just

as diamonds, have auras, on a smaller scale, of course, not as perfect—they are there nevertheless.

This proves conclusively, that fruits, minerals, animals and wherever you turn have auras, and we are able to see these auras manifesting themselves. Remember, that it is universal throughout nature; there is absolutely nothing in the universe which is devoid of the aura; it is of universal application. It is the aura, or some part of it, which we see projected in the different parts of the air; they really are the doubles, and everything of that kind. You must bear in mind the aura contains the very essence, the very being of the being himself. No matter what the condition may be, it contains his mind, it contains also the very essence of his physical constitution. Consequently, if a person is sick his aura is diseased. It is not only diseased, but the specific disease, that he has, in a word, it has the spirit of that particular disease, and the great danger of infection is not in the bugs, bacteria, etc., it is in the aura, the spiritual emanation from the body of the sick person. The odor from the sick person is far more dangerous than all the germs in the world. The odor which comes from the sick person is really his aura. That is the thing, that we must avoid above everything else. A healthy person's aura contains the very spirit of health and good or bad, or whatever his character may be, is contained in it likewise.

But the aura of a man is electrical, that of a woman is magnetic; that sex principle is in operation throughout the aura; wherever you turn, you will see that it is in a state of constant operation, of constant manifestation. Now, falling in love, when it is genuine, is nothing in the world, but the polarizing, but the uniting of the masculine and the feminine, so the two polarize and become one. Affinity is simply when two auras, which are mutually positive and negative, unite. Divorce is when this affinity ceases to exist. The auras no longer polarize; thus they are separated. When a person becomes self-sufficient the aura is both positive and negative, therefore it does not require anything, but is self-sufficient—both the poles are found within. But in either case, remember the aura is sexed. Remember that the principles of the woman are magnetic and those of the man are electric.

Now, there is no greater piece of nonsense in the world than the talk some people have, that while the physical is electric, the astral is magnetic. That is all tomfoolery. The feminine spirit, causal, mental, body, life, physical and etheric double are all feminine. Those principles of the masculine are all masculine and so continue until we reach the point of sexual polarity within ouselves and both the sexes are developed, those principles have received their sex, and this fact may be recognized by a careful examination of the aura.

One who is able to study these things can verify for himself or herself, the truth of what we say. There is no truth in the opposite. The Aura is, therefore, the outflowing of the inner person of the being.

LESSON V

DYNAMICS

This lesson deals with the sixth sense, or the dynamic sense. This dynamic sense is that activity of the muscles, when they have become so sensitively developed, that we are able to feel and sense the weight of psychical influences as they act on the muscles.

To illustrate: A muscle is capable of only two motions, contraction and relaxation. Where the fibres run in one direction the muscles are, therefore, capable of only a backward and forward motion, moving in a line. Those muscles where the fibres cross and recross, however, are able to move in two lines. Now, let us see what that implies, psychically. Anything which causes the muscular fibre to contract or shorten, moves the muscle accordingly; anything, on the other hand, which will make it relax will make it lengthen and move it accordingly. Remember, that as the degree of sensitivity in a muscle is, so will be the degree of its contraction and relaxation. All muscular action is the result of emotion, because thought manifests itself in emotion, acting upon it. Whatever this activity is; it is the result of stimulus, given the muscle because of thought, emotion, etc. The muscle is continually contracting and relaxing just as you are thinking and feeling. What we want you to understand, is, that every thought and every emotion, which passes through your mental and astral vehicles exercises an influence upon the muscular activity; that vibration is taking place in the muscular structure, the muscles are responding. The stimulus is given to the

(39)

muscle, although it may not cause it to move according to that stimulus. The physical body is, therefore, but the vibrating machine which expresses the impulse, imparted by the mind and heart, and as is the degree of sensitivity in the muscle, so will be the degree of its response to such stimuli.

Now, you will understand then, that there is a vast range of our thought and our feeling, to which the muscle does not respond, because it is not sufficiently plastic to give response to that impulse, our bodies being much more gross than our higher principles. There is, therefore, only a limited range of our feelings and our emotions to which our muscular structure will actually respond, owing to its grossness. The more sensitive this structure becomes, the more thoroughly will it respond to impulse. Consequently, the greater will be the range of vibratory impulses to which the muscles will respond which, in a word, will be duplicated through the muscular structure. Now, it is not only true, however, that our thoughts and our emotions influence our muscles that way, but the muscles themselves are able to respond to the same vibratory forces from the outside. Now, the clairo-dynamic power is that power of the muscles, that degree of sensitivity, which will cause them to respond to the vibratory impulses from the outside world, so that we can feel, not through the nerves, but through the muscles, and it will, therefore, be a more powerful feeling. We can feel all those vibratory impulses, feeling them as they come to us in the terms of weight, and our faculties of weight are receiving the impression. We will recognize them as weight, we will have that sensation.

Not only is this true, but we can take hold of a person's hand in the clairo-dynamic sense and feel his

muscles, his muscular contraction and relaxation. Therefore, it is nothing in the world but a sensitive state of
the muscles which enables them to feel and take notice
of motion of which the ordinary muscle would not take
notice at all. Understand, therefore, that the clairo-
dynamic sense is nothing in the world but a sensitive
state of the muscles, which will enable them to respond
to a very fine vibration, also a highly-developed condition of the organ of weight and the cerebellum. This is
all there is to this sense, and if we are able to succeed in
displacing the spiritual darkness, which has accumulated
around all of those physical faculties, and show a physical basis for them, they are no more wonderful than
sight and hearing, than anything else, but are simply a
more highly developed and more sensitive state of the
very same senses. Clairvoyance is no more soulseeing
than ordinary sight is; one has just as much to do with
the soul as the other.

Now the muscles become so delicately trained, that
we are able to sense things, that appear to have no body.
You have, no doubt, seen a fellow exhibiting mind-reading, showing you the wonders of mind-reading. For
instance, he has somebody conceal a knife and he agrees
to find it. His mind has nothing to do with it. It is not
telepathic at all. The fact is this: Two men go and take
the article and conceal it; then they go back and he takes
them, or one of them by the hand and starts out; they
may go at a run or they may go at a walk. If he goes in
the wrong direction, he feels the hand, or the muscles
contract, and he knows he has gone in the wrong direction. The muscles involuntarily jerk back in spite of the
man, he immediately starts in the opposite direction till
the muscles relax. He has got to keep shifting his position until he feels their muscles relax.

Suppose a pin has been inserted in a position in the wall. The same thing applies here; but simply it is muscle reading. He goes ahead and when he gets to the point where if he starts to advance any further, then the hands relax, then if he moves to the right or left the muscles contract, but where he does not move in any direction, does not feel the relaxation or contraction of the muscles, he knows that he stands immediately before the hole. If his hand starts to go up he feels the man's hand that he is holding, go down. He continually shifts the position of his hand all the time feeling the contraction or relaxation of the hand until his hand is immediately before the hole, and he does not feel any movement whatever. He is simply depending upon the muscular contraction which he feels.

This is not all. Whatever is in your mind is influencing your muscles, and where you have trained your muscles to the point where they will respond to any muscular movement in another so that when you have taken hold of a man's hand the muscular vibration will act upon you so that you will feel that muscular contraction or expansion, or the same feeling which gave rise to that muscular movement will be communicated to your mind or your astral, you will feel or think the very same emotion or feeling, you will take on his mental condition so that you can tell what he is thinking of. You do not have to have any telepathic power, whatsoever in order to do this.

Now, remember that there are two classes of dynamics, but only the simpler form will be dealt with here. We have the dynamic sense and clairo-dynamic sense. Dynamics is a really physical sense just as telepathy is a physical sense. We do not wish to go into the spiritual side. But in reference to the matter we are speaking of; here is a case in point, which will illustrate the principle; it will also illustrate the fact, that if a person has a certain thought or feeling which is constantly haunting him—a skeleton in his closet, so to speak—this will govern his thought and feeling, all the time, therefore, his muscular motion will be governed by it, and the specific fact which is in his mind is also in his muscles, so that a skeleton in a man's closet will be really revealed by his movements. There was a man in Arkansas who had a great deal of trouble with his family, and one of the Fowlers was down in that locality. He was going to give lectures and lessons on Phrenology, and he started out to canvass for his business and to become acquainted with the people. He met this old man and walked right up to him and told him his name, and shook him by the hand. Then he told the old man that he had three boys, while one was tolerably good, the other two had nearly broken him up on account of their meanness and wild actions; and it was a fact and nobody had told him. The old man's whole muscular system was always telegraphing that fact, and a person able to read or feel that sufficiently so that his mind would receive and his brain would send the impulse along the muscles, and it was nothing but muscle reading.

Graphology is nothing in the world, but the application of this dynamic law. It is known to most students of human nature that you can read character by the handwriting, but very few know the reason why you can read it by the writing. They know that a certain particular shape of a letter indicates a certain characteristic, but they do not know the reason why.

Remember, whenever you are thinking a certain thought, or a certain emotion moves you, the mental and astral body acts upon the physical, and the result is that the muscles move at a certain rate of motion owing to that impulse. It is true that motion is either one of contraction or relaxation, but they are according to the emotion or the thought; there will be so many contractions or relaxations to the second, or there will be a certain length of the contractions or relaxations, or there may be a little wavering motion, and it may not be continuous. Now, as we have this gentle wavering motion, or the violent, whatever it may be, this motion of the muscles is the result of the thought or feeling. As there are no two thoughts and no two emotions which have exactly the same vibratory effect, consequently, no two will have the same effect upon the muscles. There will be a muscular motion corresponding to the astral or mental nature, provided the muscle is able to respond to it. Therefore, as you think, your hands are moving in that way. This will add a certain quiver to the hands. The fingers are not still, the muscles are vibrating so that the finger feels a certain quivering motion, which is the result of those various muscular movements which are stimulated by the thought and by the emotion. Therefore, if there is a certain trembling in your hand the pen will tremble too, the pen will make that same trembling movement that your fingers do, consequently the pen will be duplicating all the time the thought and the emotion. Consequently there is not a person on earth who holds a pen steady; it is an utter impossibility; and that tremble makes the difference in the formation of a letter. You can, therefore, by looking at writing, tell, if you know how, just what was in that man's mind at the time he wrote, for you see the formation of the letter, and you know that there would be only required a certain emotion and certain thoughts to impart that particular tremble. Now, a Graphologist will read a person's character by noting the formation of the letters, and he usually requires thirty or more lines as a sample of a person's handwriting. Now, he can see those various characteristics. Those characteristics which are brought out in practically every word in the thirty lines without varying would be your character. If the person is thinking certain thoughts all the time while he is writing thirty lines of manuscript, those lines are likely to be the representatives of his dominating thoughts, the thoughts of his life, and whatever the person's dominant thoughts are in life, that will be his character. Consequently, seeing all the samples of writing, seeing those particular movements which are duplicated all the way through, you can see the mean motion of that man's muscles, and by seeing that you know the mean of his thought and emotion, and are able to read his character. Graphology is, therefore, nothing in the world but the reproduction of the muscular movement by the pen—the pen being the channel which connects the movement of the muscles with the writing. It is, therefore, proof that the muscles do respond to the mental and astral vibrations, and as they so respond, as this response is taking place, it follows as a logical result that the whole principle of dynamics is true.

Now, the dynamic sense is a real sense just as much so as feeling or anything else; it is the power of the muscles to sense weight. Now, what is weight anyhow? What is it that determines the weight of an article when we speak of an article as being heavy or light? Remember, before there were any scales our ideas of lightness and heaviness were formulated; before we had any mechanical devices that measure such weight. You stoop down and pick up an article; what is it that enables you to lift that? The muscles in the arm. The muscle is

perfectly relaxed when the arm is straight; the muscle
shortens and contracts, and thus we gradually raise anything up. It is not that our arm contracts, but our
muscles contract. It is by the shortening of the arm
that the muscles contract. Therefore, the difference between a heavy article and a light one is the different
degree of stimuli, which it will take to make that muscle
contract under that influence. Thus you see, this is pull-
ing the muscle out, lengthening it, and our will is shortening it. The difference then in the weight of articles is
the difference in the vibratory stimula which it will take
to shorten the muscle; that is all. And if it were not for
this there would be no difference in the weight of
articles. Scales have been introduced and they really
apply the same principle. The most primitive form of
scales is the balance. You place a certain weight in one
of the cups of the balance, and then you put in something
which you want to weigh until it balances, this weighs as
much as the weight does. You can see it is precisely the
same principle, the article weighs as much as the force
it displaces. Other methods of weighing have been introduced which are much better calculating devices.

In the study of dynamics we must bear in mind that
it is the ability of the muscles to contract or relax owing
to the two influences which are brought to bear, and
thus it is a real genuine act of weighing the impulse. We
weigh articles by the muscles in this way, because we
find that certain influences weigh more than others do,
that is, they will produce a greater degree of muscular
contraction, while others do not weigh so much it is true
they do not affect the muscles so much; and it is in this
way that we are able to tell the difference between those
forces according to their weight.

The faculties of weight may become so highly developed that we can pick up a physical object and guess how much it weighs; that is one of the activities of the faculty of weight. It gives you the power to weigh in pounds and ounces without any scales. Simply by using our faculty for that purpose we can look at an object and tell how much it weighs—at any rate we can develop that faculty. It also extends to those metaphysical forces and influences, and communicates to their intelligence the result, it communicates their character as a result of this study of their different characteristics, because it communicates to the intelligence the difference between one thing and another. It communicates, to a certain extent, the nature of the different influences by reason of the degree of contraction or relaxation which they exercise upon the muscles. It is, therefore, a sense in the most physical sense of the term. A physical sense is simply that power of being which enables the mind to become cognizant of exterior influences, that function of the body which will communicate exterior influences to the mind in order that it may know and recognize them. This activity is what constitutes a physical sense.

In the light of this you can readily see that the dynamic sense which is exercised by the trained muscle reader is nothing in the world but a purely physical sense. What is required is a more sensitive and a more highly organized state of the gross physical body. With such a state of development, we will be able to recognize these higher states; we will be able to weigh with our muscles, thought, emotion and everything else of that kind. And then we have, in the dynamic sense a true sense which deals with the relative weight of objects, both physical and even those of higher character as well; but, of course, not those of the spiritual, but those finer mental impulses which are of a higher rate of vibration than would be included under the head of the physical, because, in that case, it is not the physical structure of the muscles which responds.

LESSON VI

TELEPATHY

Telepathy literally means "feeling at a distance," but this is not strictly the sense in which we use this term in psychological research work or occultism. The term has become associated with the idea of the projection of thought from one mind to another without any physical means of communication. Now, in order for this to take place there must be certain principles in operation. There can be no such thing as thought transference unless there be some foundation, some basis for such transmission. Now, the various schools of psychological research have tried to find the foundation for telepathy, and in this they have usually made miserable failures. There is no definitely recognized hypothesis for the explanation of this telepathic phenomena, and yet telepathy itself is accepted as being the explanation for pretty near everything. Those psychological researchers who do not wish to accept the spiritual hypothesis or accept some other conclusion which would be still more far-reaching, and yet who know it is a fact that those phenomena do occur, who are not willing to take that most insane of all hypotheses that it is owing to a deranged state of the brain; that all psychics are more or less insane, now fall upon the hypothesis of telepathy as being the fullest explanation. They really like that because it appeals to them as being the best explanation without going too far. Now, mind you, these conclusions are not reached on account of any evidence that they are true. They do not accept telepathy because there is any evidence that in certain cases telepathy is true. As to what telepathy is, they do not know and do not pretend to know. We, however, claim to be in the possession of the key of telepathy.

In the first place, thought is material, or, as the New Thought people would say, "Thoughts are things." They have a tangible existence, and may be seen by the clairvoyant and felt by the psychometrist, being material and having an objective existence, but owing to their fineness and minuteness and owing, also to the fine rate of vibration which they possess, they are not visible to ordinary physical sight. But they are tangible realities just as molecules or electrons are; they are organisms formed of mental material. We thus have a physical basis, or at least a material basis for psychic phenomena, at least for a part of that phenomena. We have telepathy founded upon material thoughts. This is the first principle, from which we must start. We must discover, in the second place that thoughts have different rates of vibration, and that the Mental matter, in the third place, entirely permeates the Physical as well as the Astral; thus we have the mental plane entirely permeating everything. Each thought, as it springs into being, sets up a rate of vibration corresponding to itself, in the mental substance; that is to say, a mental wave is set in motion in this mental world and will pass anywhere in the mental world with that definite rate of vibration.

Now, the thought is projected, and vibrates. Ordinarily it will travel only a very short distance, because its tendency is to form a circle, just as all motion tends ultimately to form circles. It is contrary to the nature of all physical activity that a vibration should go in a straight line, very far. So, you will see it is not the most commonplace thing in the world for a thought to be projected to any particular place, because as it goes out, it is likely to have a curve and travel along that circle, so that thoughts usually travel in a circle a short distance only from where they were first projected. A greater degree of force imparted to a thought will cause it to go with more velocity, and travel a wider circle. Now, the ordinary thought does not have any definite directing force back of it; it is simply thought and that is all; but under certain circumstances it may be projected so as to reach its destination.

Thoughts also obey the law of attraction and repulsion. In the thought world just the same as in the physical, objects obey the same law. We have these laws in operation. Now, what is the basis of attraction and repulsion? Well, there are two forces here. What we might term the Law of Opposition and the Law of Sympathy, or a law of Antipathy and a Law of Sympathy, are two forces which are in operation. Because of this, thoughts of opposite polarity attract, and thoughts of the same polarity repel. Therefore, all electrical thoughts will repel each other, or all magnetic thoughts will repel. Electrical and magnetic thoughts mutually attract. The thoughts of the same general character, but not of the same pole, are mutually drawn together because they are friendly. There is a condition of friendship which exists among those thoughts which have the same general character; and as you know, thoughts have character the same as people have; that is, in the same way, and may be classified pretty much the same as human beings can be. You will find there are people whose ideals we approve and whose general character is what we like. We like their company. Then there are other people who are just as uncongenial, and we

shun them. Some thoughts like each other's company,
and some do not. The result is that certain thoughts
are getting together, grouping themselves together.
Now, it is very difficult to prevent a thought from seeking congenial company, just as most men would rather
meet "Hale fellows well met" and have a good time,
than go ahead and do some disagreeable duty. So a
great many thoughts object to living where fellows are
doing a disagreeable duty.

Now, it may be wise to project a thought to a certain
party. Perhaps he is uncongenial; a party whom you
do not like. The thought will be repelled by his aura, but
at the same time there will be some thoughts which will
be perfectly congenial to it. You must overcome the
decided partiality to those particular thoughts it is coming into contact with along here. So you have, in a word,
overcome those conditions to project a thought.

We must bear in mind that there are three types of
telepathy, which combine into forming four distinct
classes of communication. The first is what we might
term "Spontaneous telepathy"—but owing to the fact
that your mind is in harmony with another mind, you
have the same keynote, so to speak, which renders the
two minds responsive to each other. Your minds work
on the same key. Therefore, when you are thinking
you are positively in the same line of thought and the
other mind is negative to that particular line of thought.
If that is true, telepathy is quite likely to occur without
being sought by either party. Therefore, it is quite
likely that the thought of one will be transmitted to
the other, and this spontaneous telepathy is responsible
for a good many dreams, and a great deal of inspira-
tional ability, speaking and writing. It is not spirits at
all, but simply thoughts coming from the minds of

others. Particularly is this true when a person may be writing—may write a book, and before publication a number of people may be preaching what is in that book, etc. Now, it is very clear that we are not borrowers from them, because of the fact that what they teach is usually something that we have improved upon. It is an echo, it is what we thought six months or a year before they were giving expression to it. The spiritual hypothesis is not sound. We have the same guides and these guides are inspiring us with the same things. It is, however, a case of spontaneous telepathy. We may not get it so very clear, and in many instances the thought does not reach us until long after.

Now, when we look into the matter a little more deeply we see that this spontaneous telepathy is occurring all the time, and is, in reality the explanation of thousands of different phenomena for which physics has no explanation. But there are thousands of phenomena which it does not explain, cannot explain, because it is not the true explanation.

Now, there is the second type, which we will take up, and that is Positive Telepathy. That is to say, you want to communicate your thought to a certain party. Well, in order to do this, you must project that thought with sufficient force that it will overcome all the antagonistic influences which would drag it somewhere else, will overcome its own reluctance and will overcome any obstacle in his Aura, will force it into his Mental Body, and so the impression will be made up into his brain. If you want to use telepathy in this way it isn't necessary to go through any vigorous heroics. The best way is to sit quietly, or lie down, and you will find it is better to close the eyes, relax all the muscles; you should be perfectly relaxed while sending communications. Then, do not be so vigorous in shutting your eyes, but simply concentrate all your attention upon what you are doing by removing the attention from everything else. Simply think about so and so. A good way to do is to form in mind the picture of the person sitting before you—see him just as he is, and as he sits there, have a kind of mental conversation, thinking the thought you want to send, in exactly the same way you would talk to him, seeing him and transmitting those thoughts, and he will get them.

Another method is to see the party a long distance from you, instead of having him sit before you, and imagine that you are looking into the window of the house, trying to see him at that time under his circumstances; send your thought in the same way as given before.

Another method is to make a tube, form an imaginary eye-tube, and while looking through this, see an imaginary picture of the party at the end of this tube, just as if that picture were set up in the end of the tube; and while you are thinking of this (rather while you are seeing this) begin to tell him what you want to talk about to him. If you don't want to use this method simply think the thoughts. But it is always better if you can conjure up the picture before you. This seeing the party will help to direct the thoughts to that particular party; and do not allow them to go astray. And by projecting the thought with a good deal of force, the more positive at the time of such projection the greater will be the force which this thought will have as it reaches the party to whom it is sent. Also, it is a good idea to vitalize the thought; the thought is better to be vitally charged. In this way the person to whom it is sent, whom you are trying to communicate with, will feel it more forcibly, because it is charged,—is a working force.

Another splendid method: Concentrate your feelings, feel toward a certain person, to bring that relation —to think of him in a certain relation to yourself, and then send forth your thoughts with the strongest possible feeling.

Another type of telepathy is what we will call negative telepathy. That is just the reverse to the positive. You do not so much want to transmit thought to a party as you want to get his thought. You, therefore, become intensely negative. You listen to a conversation. You may have his before you and use all the other methods, only you have him talking to you; you listen and you make yourself negative; you cause all the vibratory forces of your aura to flow into your center of listening, and in time you will acquire that power to draw to you the thoughts of the party under consideration. This isn't so very difficult if you stop to think what proportion of his thoughts are leaving his aura and going out into the mental planes. In that case you don't have to take them away from him. You simply have to direct the course they must take after they leave the party who projected them. If you are able to do this, you will be able to catch the thought, and the more of this you do the greater will be your power to accomplish more of the same result.

Another type or class of communication is where both the positive and negative are combined, where two parties, for instance, are communicating telepathically, and are both conscious of the fact that they are doing this. Then, in that case, they must have certain hours that they will communicate, and so they will simply sit down and send strong thought projections, each to the other.

Now, if the other feels this, he will himself become negative, when he begins to think of the other party. He should immediately become negative and listen, and if he gets a certain impression, answer it. So that, in this way, it will be possible to carry on conversations with the long distance effect; in fact, over thousands of miles, intelligent conversations may be conducted if the party will answer questions, being perfectly positive, and as soon as he has said his say, become intensely negative, and listen for the answer. You can even send letters telepathically. That is to say, you can sit down and concentrate your mind and think a letter instead of writing it. The other party as soon as he begins to feel or to get impressions and becomes convinced that you are trying to communicate with him, will be intensely negative as long as he catches any thought; and will then answer the communication. It is as if one should write a letter and not send it; the other would write a letter, giving the answer and it were found that they exactly coincided word for word. Sometimes you write a letter and do not mail it. But yet it is possible that the exact words will be sent, nevertheless. Whether you send the letter or not, the impression will be a literal statement of what it contains. It is even possible for pictures to be telepathically sent. It is possible to have a picture in mind and an artist get the impression and duplicate it. Now, a case of that kind came up some three years ago. A man wrote a story, and in the hero of this story he had in mind a certain character in the city where he lived, as the prototype of this character which he brought out in the story. The story was sent to the illustrator, who was not acquainted with either the writer or the character, but was a stranger to both. To illustrate the story he was to make a picture of this man, the

hero of the story; when the picture was sent it was discovered to be an exact duplicate of the face and person
whom the author had in mind at the time the story was
written. This cannot possibly be anything but a vind-
ication of teleapthy, and there are thousands and thousands of other cases which might be cited to demonstrate
the fact that telepathic communications do actually tran-
spire.

Now there are, of course, cases where it is necessary
to have the communication going on at the same time;
that is to say, it may be necessary to have the two parties sitting at regular intervals of time and at exactly
the same time, in order that they may send their telepathic communications. In certain instances this will
be necessary; but for the highly developed telepathist,
the master, in fact, it is not necessary. Masters who have
worked along that line, who make a specialty of telepathic work, may sit down and get communications from
parties at will, because they feel the very moment when
some one is asking to get in communication with them.
In that way, this higher form of telepathy is to think of
some person and intensely desire to receive a communication from him or for him to receive one from you, and
in this way the communications may be quite easily
secured. And we will find that as those communications
are secured, it will become possible for those persons
who have the power sufficiently developed to communicate just as freely as they could with a telegraph instrument or anything else.

The time will come in the history of the world when
telepathy will be so thoroughly developed that it will
take the place of means of communication, when there
will be no instruments of telegraphy, but everybody will
resort to telepathy as it will be more rapid. All the work

will be carried on in that way. For those persons not able to transmit and receive, there will be professional operators who will simply use their power to project thought for those who cannot do it themselves. The whole system is one which is perfectly applicable to all the problems of life. There is absolutely nothing that you cannot accomplish through the activity of mental powers. It is a power, therefore, which may be used for the highest realization, the highest accomplishment along those mental lines, and for the realization of the subconscious of other persons, and it may be used in various other ways. It may be used for giving directions at a distance. In fact, it is almost impossible to estimate the value of telepathy. However, it is not the only force in the Universe by any manner of means, and we must not get the idea that it explains all the phenonena of life, for it does not.

LESSON VII

AKASHIC RECORDS

As each thought is generated in the mind it passes out from the Mental Body on to the Mental Plane and there remains for a considerable period of time, as a thought vibrating in accordance with the particular vibration pertaining to that quality of thought. As a result, its identity is maintained as long as it continues there. These thoughts obey the laws of attraction and repulsion, adhesion and cohesion, the same as other bodies do. Like attracts like, causing them to gather into groups, while those thoughts that are antagonistic are mutually repellent, thus aiding the formation of groups of the same general character. Likewise thoughts of opposite polarity are attracted while those of the same polarity are repelled. Those of like character are drawn together by reason of the fact that they have the same general vibration, differing in certain specific respects, but in a general way, being the same.

It may be said that thoughts, like people, love congenial company. Thus when a thought is projected on the Mental Plane it naturally associates itself with thoughts of a corresponding character.

By reason of this attraction and repulsion, due to congeniality growing out of their vibratory rates, the thoughts are grouped in a systematic manner, in fact, in accordance with a perfect musical arrangement. All those thoughts vibrating upon the first note of the mental octave gather in the lower part, in that part of the Mental Octave where the Manas vibrates upon that

(59)

note; and so with the other thoughts; they remain there active upon those sub-planes.

These thoughts constitute the Mental aspect of the Akashic Records, and when one has developed to the plane of mental consciousness, that is, objective consciousness of mental things, he is able to read these Records and thus recover the thoughts of the past. All past thought is thus brought within the range of the human consciousness; but it should be borne in mind that these records are records of Thought; they are not infallible, but merely represent the thinking of persons who have lived upon the earth in the past. They are valuable in so far as they deal with human thought, but not otherwise. All the books that have ever been written, are there; likewise all that have not been written, but have been held in mind, that have been thought out; and those records are more reliable than the written records, because they always represent one's actual thought, while the written records are quite often disguised and are not true to one's convictions. However, the Akashic Records are not to be accepted as absolutely infallible or anything of that kind. A great many persons when reading the Akashic Records see certain events, find dates, for instance and everything of that kind; they are able to reconstruct a complete story, and think they have discovered the history of the past. As a matter of fact they have discovered what somebody thought was the history of the past. Mr. Leadbeater's works are quite interesting as an illustration of this principle. Leadbeater has unearthed a number of Akashic romances, dealing with what some one has thought about the past, and he discovered those thoughts and they appeared to him as being actual history. He has put them forward as definite history. There is no greater mistake than this principle of accepting the thoughts in the Akashic Records as true accounts of past transactions. A romance may be stored up in the Akashic Records, perfectly connected, so that by beginning at the first of it you may go on and read it to the end, and yet it is no more reliable than the printed romances, being simply the dreams and visions of some one who has been allowing his mind to run away with him, whose imagination has run wild and has, therefore, built up a beautiful system of speculative philosophy in a way, arrayed in the form of a gospel; or perhaps it is gotten up merely for the purpose of amusing himself or something of that kind; but in this way, otherwise sane, serious investigators are led astray and accept fiction as substantial truth, as historical verity.

Another type of Akashic exploration is that represented by such books as the Aquarian Gospel of Jesus the Christ. This is drawn from the Akashic Records and purports to represent His real life and character. Here we have a history of Christ perfectly in harmony with the speculations of the Gnostics. All their philosophy is merely an elaboration of what is very positively stated in this work just as though it were historical truth. Now, what is more reasonable than to assume that some Gnostic, speculating on the life of Christ, etc., fixed up, in his imagination, a life of Christ in harmony with what had been taught for centuries, perhaps, at least for a number of decades, by his co-religionists as being the real character of Christ. Thus we have here a connected history, which is the elaboration of their belief. This speculative tank was tapped by the clairvoyant who wrote the Aquarian Gospel of Jesus the Christ; tapping this, he accepted it as being really truth, but it was true only in the sense of being an exact duplicate of the thoughts of others.

Thus, all those thoughts of persons in the past, all the works of criticism, the histories, biographies, etc., developed through philosophical speculation are likely to appear there, in fact are sure to appear if they have been thought out in terms of fact, as actual facts. Thus they are seen and taken down. It is almost an utter impossibility for one to distinguish the difference between historical truth and the mental images seen in the Akashic Records.

One of the activities of these Records is manifested in the phenomena of haunted houses. A person dies, for instance, is murdered in a house. His thoughts are associated with the place, so powerfully charged with his feelings and the scene of his murder is powerfully impressed upon his mind, and the same is true of his murderer and of any witnesses who may see it. The result is, the house becomes charged with these thoughts and remains under this influence for an indefinite time, perhaps for years and years afterwards. Some one lives in the house, some one who is of a sensitive mind, rather negative, even a mystic, perhaps. This one is influenced by the thoughts in the Akashic Records and sees the murder enacted before him. Many cases are cited where this has been observed. When the scene is enacted before him it is simply the influence of the thought, stimulating corresponding thoughts in his own consciousness.

Thus, as we go on, from one stage to another of the manifestation of this force, we are able to realize that it is nothing but human thought and emotion, nothing but the experiences which people have gone through and the impressions they have made upon them. Often a very sensitive person does not have to sleep in such a house, but when he enters it he gets those impressions; the impressions may be so strong that they become objectified and the person actually sees the embodiment of the thought there expressed.

One of the most powerful forms of these manifestations is the case of a person dying with a certain message on his mind, something he wants to tell, something he wants done. When he is in this state of consciousness he will intensely long for some one to get this, so that this message will be impressed upon the mental atmosphere of the house, and anybody living there, even anyone coming into the house is quite likely to see an apparition of the man, because his personality was associated with his thought, creating a Thought Form, the exact duplicate of himself, and this apparition will speak, insisting upon the carrying out of this wish. The words appear to come from his lips, but in reality they are merely the thought impressing itself upon the mental consciousness of the party, acting precisely the same as telepathy, only telepathy is ordinarily between the minds of two living persons. This form of telepathy is the thought impressing itself upon some one, while the person who projected it is, in most cases, long since dead. The thought simply obeys the law of attraction, and exercises its influence thus, in conformity with the mental laws, acting as a suggestion to the mind of the one who is receiving it. The majority of apparitions are due to the activity of these Akashic records.

A great deal of the inspiration many people claim is simply because of the Akashic Records acting upon their subjective consciousness. On the Mental Plane thoughts are things, in fact they are living entities and when one is able to enter into the mental consciousness he is influenced by them. He gets the thought, and if he is clairvoyant on the Mental Plane he sees the thought, not as a thought (that is if he is able to read the Akashic

Records) but as the thing which the thought represented. If he sees the thought relating to an event, he
sees the event just as though he were a spectator of it.
If it relate to an action that the person thinking it
witnessed or experienced, or even one he was thinking
about without having ever had any experience with the
action, the action will appear just as though it were
actually performed before him. Thus the history of the
past is seen as past history, not as thought about it. It
comes in a panoramic scene before one's vision and
when one sees those things he should realize that they
are merely mental images, quite as reliable as any other
human thought, but no more so.

The Devachan that Theosophists talk so much about,
is nothing in the world but this realm of thought. It has
no objective reality any more than simple thoughts have.
Of course, in a certain sense, all thought is really objective. It does not mean that it is merely what some one
thinks about Devachan, for Devachan has an objective
reality in so far as the seer is concerned. He is actually
seeing something, but its objective reality depends upon
the subjective activities of others in the past. Devachan
is, therefore, merely an elaborate Thought Form, built
up by the thinking of millions of people for thousands of
years. Their ideas have gone together to construct this
vast affair, and when they look into it, they see there as
objective realities, the thinking of persons in the past.

The visions of heaven which the Christian Seers have
seen, are nothing but their own vision of the thoughts of
others. In proof of this it is only necessary to state that
heaven is always in harmony with theology. We never
find among these seers visions of heaven that are not
strictly in conformity with the opinions of philosophers
before any such visions were seen. Not only is this true,

but they are usually in harmony with the theology of the person who is seeing them, for the reason that the Christian Seer is not in sympathy with the thoughts of a Buddhist or a Brahman philosopher, therefore, is not likely to see their Devachan. Thus one is seeing objectively the subjective heaven of Devachan of others in the past. The Catholic sees the saint in heaven; the Protestant never sees him; a Catholic never sees any heretics in heaven. So you may go on ad infinitum. You will find that the seers have seen what their predecessors believed, thought, imagined.

Again, there are many seers who are at the same time positive thinkers, such as Emanuel Swedenborg, whose thoughts were so powerful that, to him, they became objective realities, and he beheld his own creations, his own thoughts, as actualities. Thus we find the seership of Swedenborg going along in exact proportions to his philosophy. Swedenborg saw just what he had preached for years and years as being true. We see him going to heaven and there talking to the angels, arguing theology with them, pointing out some of their mistakes, even, showing them where they were wrong on a number of points. It is perfectly plain that it was simply the musing and dreaming of Swedenborg objectified. Again we see that all his experiences in heaven were simply the expression or the confirmation of his theories in the past. He believed certain things and in his experiences there he saw them verified. Likewise, his declaration of the angels being the perfected spirits of persons who had lived on the earth, is simply confirmatory of the doctrine he had taught for some time. Thus he was simply seeing his own thoughts objectified, and took them for objective realities.

Likewise, take the visions of hell. It has been stated

by Theosophists that the Astral Plane is the hell of the seers, the purgatory of the Catholics, and this is true. There is in the Astral world a world of imagination, of emotion, of feeling, passion, fear, hate. All those feelings become there objective realities, and one possessing Astral clairvoyance of that particular type necessary to read the Records, will see the actions that would ordinarily spring from those passions, those emotions; they are usually acted out; likewise emotions become entities, and are seen. They become devils and they condemn. If one is cursing another and condemning another, forming a picture of him in a state of condemnation, that Astral picture will go through torments there. Thus one seeing the Astral Plane will behold the passions acting as live forces; consequently, there is a kind of ideal world in the Astral Plane, a world of passion or emotion which has become objective to the Seer. This is the hell that Swedenborg went through, and all his descriptions of heaven and hell are simply descriptions of the emotional and mental Karma on the Astral and Mental Planes, these shadows of the Akashic Records, and when we realize that they deceived so grand a philosopher and so great a seer as Swedenborg, it is not at all surprising that many should mistake them for the higher Akashic Record.

Now, on the Buddhic Plane there is a Record not dependent upon thought or feeling, but a record built up by the pure reason. The truth discovered by the pure reason there becomes objective, and inasmuch as the pure reason is employed in the discovery of the truth and truth only, those pictures are perfectly correct. They also represent forces and principles perfectly accurate, and those records are reliable so far as all material things are concerned. The picture represents action, reason and principle, and is a faithful transcript of all those things cognized through the intuition and built up through the pure reason. Systems of philosophy and metaphysics perfectly in harmony with truth are stored up there, the only books to be found there being books teaching absolute truth. There are no errors in those records. One in possession of Buddhic clairvoyance will be able to read that record. Reading that record, he will be able to learn the truth about material things and about the history of the world so far as the material is concerned; but here we are presented with a difficulty. Many people think because this is true they should be able to tell how long it has been since the events transpired. They think the Akashic Records will give them dates, but this is a great mistake. The Astral Record deals only with what people have felt about things; the Mental Record only with what they have thought about them; the Buddhic or true Akashic Record, does not deal with time at all. It takes no cognizance of time or space, but deals with absolute truth; therefore, you will find there a record of what has transpired, but you will find no way to indicate when it transpired. The only way to form any idea of time on this Plane is by observing the sequence of events; seeing what happened before and after a given event, and by tracing out the sequence, you will be able to tell with a certain degree of accuracy somewhere near when it transpired. One of the favorite methods for determining when an event occurred has been to look around and see if you could not find some historical character whom you could recognize there and when you recognized him, you would know it was during his life time. But this is very inaccurate. In the first place, if you are on the Mental Plane you are just as likely as not to see a character that did not exist at all;

some person like Sherlock Holmes, The Count of Monte Cristo, etc., as you are to see a person who actually had an historical existence, and again, you are likly to see an historical character who is there, not because it was in his lifetime, but because the one who was doing the thinking had him associated in his mind with that historical event as he was thinking about it, the whole foundation of these appearances being mind. Likewise a poetical effusion may cause the appearance of some one in the Astral Record, the Buddhic Record being the only one that is reliable, but on the Buddhic Plane if the reason is associating the principle with some great personality, he is likely to appear even there.

Another thing: very seldon do forms of people appear on the Buddhic Plane at all, and when they do, they owe their existence to the reason more than to objective existence. A person may use them in his reason as an illustration, a symbol of the principle he has in view, and if the pure reason deals with them in this way, they will appear on the Buddhic Plane.

Thus it appears that there is no very great degree of accuracy in any of the methods employed for the purpose of measuring time by the Akashic Records, though we can recover principles, truth, thought and emotion. They are not, consequently, of so much historical value, but of great philosophical and literary value. When it comes to the study of the history of philosophy, there is nothing so valuable as these records, but they must never be assumed to represent a perfect system of history when it comes to dates. Otherwise, however, the Records on the Buddhic Plane are quite valuable for historical purpose.

LESSON VIII

CLAIRVOYANCE

Clairvoyance means literally "Clear seeing." But there are four or five phases of clairvoyance. For instance, one type, the type to see backward, looking backward and seeing things that have happened long ago; another type, that of seeing in the future, things that are going to happen hereafter. And the third type is, looking off and seeing things happening somewhere else in the world at a considerable distance; the fourth type, the capacity to see things which are in their nature, invisible; that is, objects which are not visible to ordinary sight.

It is the fourth type of clairvoyance that is divisible into a number of subdivisions. Let us see if we can ascertain the foundation of clairvoyance, and then we will be able to bring these matters into our consciousness.

In the first place, we have to recognize the fact that there are lights too bright to be seen. We do not see certain lights and colors—not because they are not there, but because they are so bright we can not see them. You know that vibration works at different rates, and different colors vibrate so many vibrations to the second. Now, the optic nerve is capable of responding to a certain number of vibrations per second. Below that range there is a minimum and above that range there is a maximum range of optic response. Below that number of vibrations per second always darkness. We do not take cognizance of an object which is vibrating below that rate. Then we go upward an immense scale of vibrations that the optic nerve will take cognizance of. At last we come to vibrations which are so high that the optic nerve will no longer respond to them, and it will not communicate any message to the brain. Now, in sight the optic nerve responds to the vibration of the crystalline lenses of the eye. Light falls on the crystalline lens and causes it to vibrate in response to the vibrations of the energy which comes in contact with it. This crystalline lens acts upon the optic nerve, the tremor to the nerve center of sight, which is located in the brain, and thus acts upon the organ of vibration, and the vibration is thus communicated to brain cells along the brain fibre, and they respond; the result is, that the object from which that vibration came, is duplicated, and there is a sensation the same way. It is a kind of telegraphy taking place, and we become conscious of that object, whatever it may be, that transmitted that vibration, not as an idea but as an object, not as a thought but an object. As that is the rationale of thought, we find that by applying this thought rationale to clairvoyance we will be able to understand the fourth type quite easily.

If the optic nerve responds to a rate of vibration and communicates this vibration to the brain we will see the object. But if it does not respond to this rate of vibration then we do not see it. The result is that there is a great field which is invisible; not because it is not there, but because our seeing apparatus is defective, is limited. We cannot see beyond those limitations.

Now, if we can make our optic nerve and our brain centers more sensitive so that it is finely organized and is capable of responding to a higher rate of vibration we will thus be able to extend the horizon of our sight so that we can see things which before were invisible. Now, all there really is in the development of clairvoyance is to make the centers more sensitive so that we extend our power of sight until we can see the invisible.

Let us see; suppose we go into a large room, and we take with us a candle. In this room, at night, we can see a few of the objects by the light of the candle but they are not very clear. There is a circle of objects here which can be seen. That is all. Now we bring in a kerosene lamp; the light becomes stronger. We see more. This kerosene lamp represents the sight that comes when we have made our nerves more sensitive so that they are more capable of sensing a more extended range of vibration. But bye and bye we light a gas jet and we see that there is a much larger range of vibration visible than at any other time. This visibility is extended to a great degree. Now, this gas jet represents this: when the etheric double has become associated with the brain, and body, and so forth that this entire double will respond to the vibration that comes into contact with any etheric vibration, is carried there to the center of consciousness, this is what is termed Etheric Clairvoyance. We can see objects which are not on the gross physical plane, but which are etheric. We can see, for instance, the ultimate physical atom. We can see electrons, and we can see the atoms and molecules more clearly; perfectly plain, because the etheric double now communicates all etheric vibrations to the brain centers. When we are here we can look through solid objects; we can see through a solid wall, and see what is on the other side. We will see —like a looking glass perspective, everything invisible from its true relation. We find this imaginery. Turn on an incandescent lamp and the light becomes brighter. We see much farther and we see a greater range of objects. And this represents astral clairvoyance, when the astral body becomes so attuned to the brain, that it will communicate any vibration of astral matter. We can then see the images, the pictures which are on the astral plane, imagery, the passions, the desire, the lusts of people. We can also see life energy and the ultimate astral atom, and we can see the astral shells of people which have been left after their death; and, in fact, everything on the astral plane becomes visible to our consciousness because the astral body is capable of responding to those vibrations to which the physical body and the etheric double cannot respond, and it communicates them to our consciousness, and we thus become conscious of those objects. But at last the party turns on, we will say, an electric arc lamp, which makes everything much more luminous, than it was before, and we can see a greater range of objects. This represents the time when the Mental Body becomes in a higher state, and also the Causal Body becomes the vehicle of consciousness. It communicates vibrations responding to it, which are carried into the consciousness and there create the impression. We can see thought forms, and thought vibrations. We are thus able to read Akashic records, because they are brought into ourselves, and so they are reproduced on our individual consciousness; and having entered into this state, this condition, we are able to realize those forces, those energies which are brought into our consciousness. But, at last, the sun rises and the man *sees,* the room is illuminated, and he sees everything that is in it. This represents the time when the Buddhic body, or the soul principle, becomes so delicately attuned to the soul world, or Buddhic, that the vibrations from the Buddhic plane are communicated through this Buddhic body and he sees everything as it is. He becomes conscious of all nature around him and thus he sees those objects; the vibratory impulse is reproduced in his consciousness. But, bear in mind that those higher forms of clairvoyance do not act through observation simply, but the organ of Human Nature, Intuition, which is the seat of Seership, working in conjunction with the pineal gland; it is the Third Eye, the eye of seership.

Now, in Buddhic clairvoyance, the Buddhic body works in connection with this, and the pineal gland, so that in this way the soul vision, or seership, is awakened. while in the mental clairvoyance the pineal gland is not awakened; the organ of human nature is the center through which it operates, the astral clairvoyance—partly that and partly the organ of observation, and in this way the consciousness of surrounding objects along those planes is realized. In Physical Clairvoyance we could see through an object by seeing everything backwards. In astral clairvoyance we are able to see everything as it really is; that is, we are able to see the molecules separate, severally in their positions.

Now, by Mental Clairvoyance we see those molecules divided into atoms; we can see the atoms of the molecules separately. We can thus get right in the middle of that molecule, and see everything in that, in its true relation, and in the Buddhic clairvoyance we are able to get into the atom and see all the ultimate atoms that compose it. And thus we see the ultimate physical and ultimate astral, ultimate mental and everything; and we see the composition of all those forces and are able to thus realize them in their true relation. It is, therefore, true that it is simply a question of a more sensitive state of the diverse principles of the human constitution which leads up to this higher sight, this clear seeing, and that is all there is in the matter.

Take the third type of Clairvoyance, seeing at a distance. You see something which is happening somewhere else, somewhere very far removed from you. How is it that you are able to see that? Simply because space is no limitation to vibration, and vibration is going on, and when you get so that you can respond to that vibration you will thus be able to see the thing acting out, and because that vibration which is sent forth communicates, as it were, the fancy of that action, just as it is taking place wherever it may be. Now, it depends upon the degree of development of your clairvoyant faculty about how far in space you can see. To the person who has Buddhic clairvoyance, there is no such thing as space. Space is an illusion; it has no existence, because he can see what is happening ten thousand miles away as well as what is happening within six inches of him when he is functioning upon that plane. The reason is that on the Buddhic plane, the vibrations are going through it perfectly. It is the same communication for thousands of miles as it is here at this one point, and everything in the universe, all the lower planes, are made up of Buddhic matter, and this Buddhic matter is continually vibrating. When the Buddhic body is awakened, attuned to this vibration, it senses the swell, as it were, it feels the pulse of the Buddhic heart, as we might term the Buddhic plane, and thus wherever we turn, wherever we fix our consciousness upon a certain thing we can see it no matter how far away it is; we can tell just what has happened. In a word, there is no such thing as space on the Buddhic plane; the cause of the sensation is just the same throughout the Buddhic plane. Buddhic matter quivers and throbs out every vibration that is set up. There is no resistance, nothing to check it, and we can, therefore, feel in tune with everything in the universe. Of course, if we are on the lower plane, the range is circumscribed; but still there is a limit to the extent of our sight. But it is because of this communicability of the Buddhic substance, as the case may be, that happenings are communicating the sensation, the impulse, which is sent forth by a cretain action that sets up the vibration on that particular plane, which will communicate the action, so that we will see it.

Now, in clairvoyance, seeing something that has taken place long ago, or perhaps not so long ago, we see it re-enacted. Well, this can be nderstood when you realize what we have already stated in regard to the Akashic Records. When you realize that every thought which is expressed is stored up on the mental plane, and every emotion is stored up on the Astral Plane and stays there forever. Now, if a person while doing a certain thing, while looking on and seeing certain things take place, is forming in mind a picture of what he sees, the mental picture which he forms of that happening is stored up in the Akashic Records. Now, if, for any cause, either directly or indirectly, that is, we mean subjectively, or of your own volition, you come into contact, come into that state of vibration, harmony, vibratory rapport with that picture, whether it was an emotional or an intellectual picture, in either case its vibration is communicated to the corresponding principle of your constitution, and you feel it; it is drawn inward, if you are negative; it passes inward to your consciousness, and thus you see the object. Thus clairvoyants see the things in haunted houses, see things acting. It creates such a strong influence that the sensation causes the picture to be duplicated. Now, this is the key to all past clairvoyance, because the picture is there on the astral plane or mental plane, as the case may be, and that picture is continually expressing itself in that peculiar rate of vibration which was set in motion by that thought or feeling. The result is that when it comes to you and acts upon your sight, you see it right there.

Now, how is it that you see things before they happen? This is the other type of clairvoyance. How are you going to see things before they take place? Because they have already taken place. Nothing ever "happens" on the physical until it has already happened on the Astral. What we mean is, you never do an act until you want to do it. You may say you never want to do it. You may not want to do it in the absolute, but under the circumstances, you want to do it rather than take the consequences from not doing it. Now, therefore, all action must be preceded by a corresponding feeling. This feeling will be reproduced there astrally; and being produced on the astral the vibration corresponding to it, the vibration which is generated by this feeling will continue to operate thereon; thus the person who has the power of astral clairvoyance will see this. And remember that the time the person wants to do a thing, desires it, from that time, on the astral plane it is a finished result, because it is not happenings that you see on the astral plane, but desires. Consequently if you have that clairvoyant power, you see it as an accomplished result. Now, in the course of time, desire manifests itself in action. Of course, speaking in relation to individuals, a man's desires are pretty apt to compel him to do certain things, but he does what he desires to do. But even suppose that he does not do it; this desire becomes a force which will act upon some person's desire body, and somebody else will do it. In a word, everything that happens on the physical plane is the result of feeling or emotion. Whenever you get the force in operation it is going to be reproduced on the physical plane. That is the reason that desire is such a terrible thing. You may make up your mind that you want to do something else than that; that you won't do it—that does not affect the desire effect on the astral plane. It goes right ahead and accomplishes its purpose just the same.

You know the statement. "Coming events cast their shadows before," and it is to this it has reference. Before any event happens on the physical plane it has already happened on the astral. It is there on the astral plane. The person of astral clairvoyance sees it before it takes place here. A person never desires a thing until after he has thought about it. Therefore, in the person himself the desire follows the thinker and on the mental plane thought generates a force; it sets up a vibration, and thus, if seen there, will be seen as an accomplished fact. Now, when it descends in time, this thought force will descend to the astral plane and will manifest itself in desire force. We do not mean that people who get this will desire this. We mean that this mental impulse in itself will descend to the desire world and, by acting upon this, generate a corresponding desire force; and this, in turn, will descend and generate a corresponding physical force. Therefore, when once a mental impulse is generated on the mental plane, it is capable of expressing itself on the physical plane without any further assistance from man. For instance, a man may form a mental picture of a cyclone, a tornado, or anything of the kind; a picture is capable of descending and expressing itself on the physical plane and generating an earthquake, or whatever it may be. And thus these mental disturbances are the result of past mental picturing, and everything of that kind; calamities, which people think about or prophesy, are very likely to express themselves on the physical plane to manifest in the

form of what was just expected, what was being looked
forward to. Now, if this manifestation is the result of a
force generated on the higher planes, astral or mental,
the person who is able to function on that plane, to function throuh that principle, perceives the accomplished
result of that picture, just as it is going to be. Consequently he will see an event before it happens, from
a few minutes to a year or two, maybe two or three
years, if on the astral plane. If on the mental plane, he
will see it perhaps a number of years up to a century
before it happens. But in terms of years it is seen on
the mental plane. The higher up it is on the mental
plane the longer it takes to descend. If a man is able
to enter on the Buddhic plane he sees the pure Kosmic
forces in operation there, and thus he will see the force
which is operating on the mental plane. He sees the
great Kosmic forces which are directing the activities
of the great physical forces, and seeing that Kosmic
force, he sees the effect that it is going to have because
of the fact that it is going to have the materialized expression of it, and in that case he can see centuries
beforehand. And if he is able to have Nirvanic Clairvoyance, he will be able to see an event thousands of
years ahead; because he then sees the spiritual forces
which are back of all things, back of all those forces,
the spiritual force which is really the governing force
of the world. Understand, it isn't the Nirvance; but the
Para-Nirvanee, the one whose spirit is perfectly attuned
to the universal spirit. Now, if he reaches the stage
of Maha-Para-Nirvanic Clairvoyance, he can see the
purposes of the Divine, the purposes which God has
sent forth, and he can see what God is going to do before
He does it. This is the higher record of God's remem-
brance, and a few can see this when their spirits come

into harmony with Maha-Para-Nirvana, or a few stages
before that. And we realize then that seeing into the
future is simply seeing into the past on a higher plane.
Then we can understand the rationale of seership;
seership is perfectly rational, perfectly scientific, when
we realize that it is simply seeing on a higher plane,
and we can realize that the things are bound to happen
on the physical plane sooner or later, and in time we
can calculate about how long it will take for it to
descend. Thus we are able to see into the future, and
this is the secret of clairvoyance in the future. It is,
therefore, all the way through merely a matter of sensation, merely a matter of becoming more sensitive so
that we are able to see those forces. When we realize
that a person's character, and everything of the kind,
all his feelings, and all those things express themselves
in corresponding rhythm, then we can understand why
it is that the clairvoyant is able to tell accurately the
character of a person; he is able to look at a person's
astral, he is able to see those colors and every emotion
of the person's character, or what those colors indicate.
We know that clairvoyance is not telephathy. Ninety-
nine out of every hundred persons who have this power
don't know what the symbols, figures, geometrical figures that they see mean. It isn't an intellectual process,
therefore; it is not a communication to the mind of
certain thoughts. They don't know what is the meaning
of what they see. It is, therefore, a chemical process.
Now, we find it depends upon a sensitivity of those
principles for the reason that there are drugs which
will stimulate those principles until clairvoyance becomes a fact; a person may become a clairvoyant from
inhaling gas. The Hindu fakers and others produce a
clairvoyant condition by using hasheesh and opium, and

other drugs. Others, by suppressing the breath and the carbon will have the effect of stimulating the same principles, so that they are awakened. Morphine and all those drugs have the same effect, and a man may drink alcoholic liquors until he becomes very sensitive and the result is he sees things, as in the case of delirium tremens, they are actually there and he simply sees them. It is a fact, then that a person should not see those things until he reaches a higher development all along the line.

Also, there is trance clairvoyance. It is produced in dreams. People concentrate until they bring themselves into this trance condition. This trance simply elevates the principles to a more sensitive condition than is ordinarily the case. There is the subjective trance and ecstasy. In ecstasy we elevate ourselves above the ordinary planes of consciousness. That was the case of Paul when he was caught up into the third heaven and heard unspeakable sounds or words which it is not lawful for man to utter. But in this state of exaltation he was able to come into contact with those principles and he saw away into the future. On the other hand, we have the subjective trance. When the mind is paralyzed, when the objective faculties are paralyzed and put to sleep we can see those things in that condition. This is the type which is found among spiritualists. The hypnotic influences and the astral faculties are highly excited and thus they are able to see.

Another form of hypnotism—spiritualistic trance, or control, is simply hypnotism by a spirit. The medium is just as materially hypnotized as the subject is in a hypnotic circle. The only difference is that it is an entity out of the physical body, a demon, or whatever it may be, it is a non-entity, that has put itself in that condition, and so stimulated their clairvoyant faculties. Now, you see those people, in these holiness meetings, in these revivals, get under this influence and see things. This is a form of hypnotism. The emotions are brought to a high degree of excitement, the astral body is highly excited and acts upon the brain, making it extremely sensitive. The things they see are purely psychical; clairvoyance may be induced all at once by a high influx of spiritual forces, spiritual energy may come in a very high degree. If this spiritual energy is concentrated properly upon the brain it may produce spontaneous clairvoyance at that time. When Elijah was on the mountain and his servant became afraid, he prayed that the young man's eyes might be opened, and they were, and he saw the mountain covered with angels. We have in this instance a case of spontaneous clairvoyance, which was induced by an outflowing, an outpouring of the Holy Spirit on this young man, Elijah's servant, so that his clairvoyant faculties were quickened, so that he was able to realize the things that were going on around him.

Clairvoyance, in all its phases, is simply a highly sensitive condition of either the physical, the etheric double, the astral or the Buddhic, or whatever it may be, so that we come into contact with those forces which are ordinarily invisible around us.

Now, how is it that the clairvoyant is able to locate gold, treasures, etc.? Simply because he is able to take notice of the vibration those metals or those minerals set up. Remember, they are really alive, they are throwing off their aura all the time, their vibration is set off all the time, acting upon the ether. The clairvoyant who is able to respond to those vibrations will see the ore, and in many instances being able to locate gems and buried treasures.

Don't spend any money trying to locate buried treasures or mineral deposits. There are plenty of them who can do this, but people who can do it are divided into two classes;—People who want money and people who don't care anything about it. If they are able to locate buried treasures, etc., instead of letting you pay them $10 to tell the secret of where to find such, or where $10,000 is buried, they will locate and get it themselves. A person who doesn't care anything about money isn't going to tell you where a treasure is. They are not going to exercise their gift of clairvoyance in that way. The very fact that they are exercising their power for money is proof positive that they like money, and if they like money, they are going to get the pot of gold themselves if they can locate it; and clairvoyants who do this are all of them fakes.

Disease may be seen while looking into the Aura because the vibration of disease is there and you may locate, if you know what it is, what those colors and symbols mean, and you can diagnose your patient, you can see those vibrations and those colors and see the evidence. You can see just what the disease is because you can see the force which emanates from it.

LESSON IX

CLAIRAUDIENCE

Clairaudience, meaning literally clear hearing, bears the same relation to the physical sense of hearing that clairvoyance does to sight. There are not only lights too bright to be seen, but also sounds too shrill to be heard. In other words, all bodies throw off an Aura, vibrating over a great range, which vibrations stimulate sight, hearing, smell, taste and feeling or touch, in those who come in contact with them, providing their centers of consciousness are able to respond to those vibrations.

The five Tattvas, which correspond to the five lower senses, operate not only on the physical plane, but on all the other planes of nature, being the five modifications of the great breath. Just as the luminiferous ether enables us to see the object from which this ether emanated, likewise does the ether of sound, the Sonoriferous Ether, enable us to sense the sound emanating from such bodies. As this sound comes to us, setting up corresponding vibrations in our Aura, we sense the same sound, if these Tattvas are sufficiently active within our principles to respond.

Hearing is really the response of the Sonoriferous Ether in our Aura to the vibrations emanating from that in the Aura of the object. This ether, causing certain vibrations to act upon the ether between this Aura and our own, develops in that ether the same vibrations. Thus the ether around us becomes the plastic medium between the Aura of the object emanating the sound, and our own Aura. The object from which the sound comes is thus the transmitter, our own Aura the receiver and the Ether the transmitting medium.

The simplest form of sound, of course, is that of the

Physical Ether. When those waves strike our Etheric Doubles, transmitting these vibrations, the quiver thus passes to that part of our Etheric Double centering in the Organ of Observation. Thus we take note of the sound. It, of course, reaches us through the instrumentality of the ear and of the auditory nerve in ordinary physical hearing, but in the case of the higher vibrations it can not do this for the reason that the auditory nerve, being physical, is not able to respond to those etheric vibrations, the result being our inability to take cognizance of the sound. But in these higher vibrations it is possible for the Etheric Double itself, that is, the Sonoriferous Ether, to respond to those vibrations, so that these Etheric currents communicate these vibrations direct to the center of hearing. Thus we are able to hear sounds of an etheric character and this includes all etheric vibrations. Any motion that is set up in the ether, thus becomes audible. The whirls generated by actions, that is, the physical actions, are thus brought into the range of our hearing, are made audible.

As we develop the Astral Body, if the Sonoriferous Ether is there developed, sensitized, brought into a state of activity, if it is so developed as to respond to the vibrations of the Sonoriferous Ether on the Astral Plane, we are enabled thereby to hear the sound of all Astral Vibrations. We can actually hear emotions, hate, everything of that kind, everything that comes into the heart of man; all his wishes, his fears, his hopes, his expectancies, become to us, audible voices. We can literally hear them speak; we can know just what they are saying, just what their message is, and as we hear them as though they were voices speaking to us, we are able in this way to come into a realization of what is transpiring on the Astral Plane. Not only can we do this, but we can hear the activities of the Astral Bodies, of all different objects, everything of the kind, in fact. This is made possible by reason of the response of the Sonoriferous Ether in our Astral Body, to the vibration of the same ether on the Astral Plane, it being the Plastic medium between the Sonoriferous Ether of the diverse Astral Bodies and that of our own.

The same principle applies to Mental Clairaudience. This is simply the development of the Sonoriferous Ether in our Mental Body to that point where it will respond to the vibration in the same ether on the Mental Plane, that being the plastic medium between the Sonoriferous Ether of other mental bodies and our own. In this way we can also hear thoughts; we do not see them, but hear them just as though they had been spoken. The thought comes not as a thought, but as a spoken word, and all the vibrations within the Mental Bodies of persons are heard. We can hear the activities of the minds of plants and rocks and everything of that kind. We can hear all those activities, but if it be only on the Mental Plane, we can hear only the Mental activities in the region of concrete thought, not those in the world of abstract thought. In order to hear the activities in the region of abstract thought, we must develop the Sonoriferous Ether in our Causal Body the same as that in the Mental Body, when it will act in the same way and bring to us the ability to hear the realm of abstract thought as well as the concrete.

All these sounds come to the Organ of Observation. The senses of the three worlds, the Physical, the Astral and the Mental, center in observation because with this faculty we become conscious of the objective world, those three worlds, in fact. But to hear on the Buddhic Plane we must develop the faculty of Human Nature or Intuition, Seership, this being the Perceptive Faculty of Buddhi.

For those three lower planes it will, therefore, appear that a highly sensitized state of the Organ of Observation is necessary, as well as a development of the Sonoriferous Ether in these different principles. Likewise, for Buddhic clairaudience, Seership must be developed and when seership is developed in conjunction with the Sonoriferous Ether in the Soul or Buddhic principle it will give the ability to hear as well as see. Seership in the sense of seeing form or anything of that kind in the clairvoyant sense is simply due to a development of this faculty in conjunction with the Luminiferous Ether of the soul or Buddhic Body, while the Soul Hearing or auditory aspect of seership, Buddhic Clairaudience, is attained through the development of the faculty of seership in conjunction with the Sonoriferous Ether of the Buddhic Body; thus we are able to hear everything transpiring on the Buddhic Plane in the same manner as we would hear sounds on the physical plane.

When the Sonoriferous Ether of the Atma or Spirit, has been developed so that it will respond to vibration on the spiritual plane, it gives us spiritual clairaudience, ability to see spiritual things, to hear the vibrations on the Spiritual Plane, and when this has been developed to a very high degree in conjunction with the faculty of spirituality, and one's spirit has become in its vibration very highly spiritualized, very much approaching to God, he, in time, is able to hear the whirl of the Divine Spirit coming forth from His fiat, as reality, so that the idea of God as well as the Kosmic idea becomes perfectly audible to him and he is able to listen to the voice of God. Likewise when his Sonoriferous Ether has been highly developed so that he is able to respond to the vibration of the world without, particularly when it has been developed along the lines of harmony and in conjunction with the development of his faculty of music he is able to hear the Music of the Spheres, this being due to a development of Music and Time in conjunction with the Sonoriferous Ether in his Aura.

But, in a general way, Clairaudience is due to a development of the Sonoriferous Ether. This is the explanation for the, too many, contradictory statements, that a person may be clairvoyant and not clairaudient; that development does not necessarily give the physical senses. The average person has an idea that it is necessary for one to have psychical powers, senses, in order to establish his spirituality; in other words, that as one becomes spiritual he will develop these senses and that if he does not have them it is evidence that he is not spiritual, while others think they must all be developed simultaneously. This is all nonsense. Clairvoyance depends upon a high development and activity, a sensitivity in the Luminiferous Ether in one's Aura, and no matter what plane he is on, unless this Luminiferous Ether is highly developed and active, although vibrating on a high plane, he will not see things; but he may have this developed ever so highly and may even become clairvoyant, and yet if his Sonoriferous Ether is not developed in the same way, he will not hear clairaudiently, for clairaudient hearing is dependent absolutely upon the development of the Sonoriferous Ether, and a person will hear only those things pertaining to the plane on which his Sonoriferous Ether is strongly operative; therefore, if one would develop a certain sense, he must exercise it, and the exercising of this is what leads to its development.

It sometimes follows that as one raises his Aura to a higher plane of vibration, all these Ethers vibrate alike; sometimes one comes before others; in fact, usually we may say in the path of development, clairvoyance comes first and then clairaudience. As we develop them, however, unless this development comes naturally, that is without effort, we are really turning our development from other channels into this particular channel. This is the reason why occultists warn their pupils against seeking for powers for psychical experiences, etc. If they seek and secure those powers, they will not be developing in other ways. The raising of the vibration will be turned into this particular channel and will thus not lead up to the spiritual state.

Further, it should be borne in mind that Physical, Astral and Mental psychism depend upon development of those three principles in conjunction with the organ of Observation, threfore, does not require any spirituality or even soul growth at all. It is for this reason that we are warned to shun the seeking for those powers, but passing them up, renouncing them, to go on until we develop Buddhi; this being from the Intuition, we shall in attaining our psychism on that plane, be able to cognize truth instead of the illusions of the three lower worlds. As we attain the cognition of truth, of course, it will help our soul growth to a certain extent. If we do not develop them through the soul, however, but pass on until we awaken the spirit, we shall find that great spirituality will be necessary, will be in fact, absolutely essential in order to such development, and then we shall be enabled to reach a much higher illumination, because it will be our spiritual hearing or sight or whatever it may be instead of those lower things, and thus what we learn through the faculties will be of a spiritual nature. It is, therefore, to prevent our being stopped on the lower planes that we are warned against seeking to develop those lower forms of Clairvoyance, Clairaudience, etc. But one who wishes to develop them, may do so by listening, by straining his hearing slightly, by trying to hear things beyond him, by fixing his attention upon the middle ear and also upon the Organ of Observation with the intention of hearing; by imagining that he is hearing things and everything of that kind. In the course of time he will be able to hear. Also, as this is obtained through a sensitizing of the whole being, it will be found that the more sensitive the body becomes, as well as the other principles, the sooner will he be enabled to hear things on those planes. Now, the physical body is sensitized by the food we eat, by eating food of a fine, sensitizing, refining, purifying quality, such as fruits, and also, to a certain extent, nuts and cereals, but no meat; nothing which grows under ground; and we sensitize the Astral Body mainly by feeling fine emotions and also, to a certain extent, by proper diet. That which feeds the Astral Body is mainly the legumes and a few other things. The Mental Body is mainly nourished by vegetables and is sensitized by thinking concrete thought of a fine quality. The Causal Body is nourished by vegetables, fruits and by thinking abstract thought and the higher we reach, the more sensitive it becomes. Buddhi is built up by reason, intuition, compassion and by living on cereals largely, while the Atma or Spirit is, of course, built up by spiritual activities to the total exclusion of everything else, by a spiritual understanding and illumination and may be nourished by a diet of fruits and nuts.

One may develop the psychical faculties by remaining quiet, sitting in the silence, by meditating a great portion of the time, keeping out of the crowd, avoiding all excitement, eating sparingly, fasting, and by avoiding all objectionable people. Also it should be borne in mind that as the gross body weakens so the activity of the higher principles increases, but, ordinarily speaking, it is not desirable to make a definite effort to develop these senses. If they come naturally, as a result of the development of those principles, as the growth of soul goes on, good and well, but otherwise they are better let alone, and one should not despair because his psychical faculties are not developed. If his spirituality, his character is developing he is much more spiritual than if he had ever so many of those physical faculties. However, they are advantageous in the same way that the physical organs are advantageous in the investigation of those higher realms so far as the physical is concerned. Adeptship, of course, requires one or more of those faculties on that particular plane in order that we may investigate the truth there.

When Clairaudience is sufficiently developed, we will be able to literally hear the grass grow, to hear the flowers and everything of that kind, hear the leaves opening, to go out into the forest and listen to it, to study botany through our auditory sense.

Sound may be quite as effective in the study of nature as it is in ordinary intercourse with humanity, when this Clairaudient faculty is awakened. There is more truth than poetry in the poem about "Little Pearl Honeydew six years old who laid her head on the strawberry bed, to hear what the red cheeked berries said." Stories about there being sermons in the running brooks and stones are absolutely correct, and we can hear them if we can only open our ears and listen to the voice which nature has for us; and likewise, when the Spiritual Clairaudience is developed and we have reached a sufficiently high degree of spirituality, we shall be able to hear the voice of God coming to us just as literally as we now hear the voice of man. The Music of the Spheres is no illusion to the one whose ear is attuned to the harmony of the Universe. These are all manifestations of the great Clairaudient Power operative through the development of the Sonoriferous Ether in our Aura.

LESSON X

PSYCHOMETRY

One of the most important of the psychical senses is Psychometry. This sense was first discovered by Dr. Buchanan, and received the name Psychometry, meaning Soul Measure, because it was considered a means by which the measure of the soul might be taken. That is, the sensitive, by handling an article magnetized by some one else, would be able to measure that person's soul.

This is th sense in which the term is used. It is, however, Psychical Touch. While Dr. Buchanan discovered it, its real nature was established more by the researches of Professor and Mrs. Denton than by anything that had gone before or has come since. Professor Denton's book, "The Soul of Things" is the best work that has ever been written on the subject. In this book Professor Denton understakes to show that not only people but things, have souls. There is nothing that is not endowed with a soul; by psychometrizing an object the soul of that object may be measured.

There is, therefore, no branch of Psychism capable of yielding such valuable results as Psychometry. It may be stated in the first place, that the Tangiferous Ether, the Ether of touch, tactility, is the channel through which we come in contact with the nature of things, psychometrically; in fact, our touch is due to the activity of this Tangiferous Ether. The Tangiferous Ether is really the etheric carbon, which becomes c a r b o n when it has descended into the gaseous state. Every object is throwing forth an Aura which contains all those Ethers within itself. As this Aura is thrown off, it generates vibrations around it; that is to say, in the plastic medium between it and the different Auras. The ether diffused about us is the plastic medium between the different Auras. As an Aura transmits a definite rate of vibration to this plastic medium, that vibration is set up there and thus passes to other Auras capable of responding to the same. In other words, this vibration comes to you, but you may not sense it. It may pass by you like water poured on a duck's back; nevertheless it reaches you. It is possible, by becoming negative, to draw to you those vibrations, while, by being positive, you can drive them from you.

As the vibration touches your own Aura, causing it to vibrate in response to the impact without, you experience the condition which was present in the Aura from which the vibration first proceeded, but it depends upon which ether it is that responds to this vibratory impact about which sense it functions through. You will not feel it unless your Tangiferous Ether responds. The other Ethers may duplicate it so that that object will present itself through other senses, but it will not present itself through the sense of Touch unless the Tangiferous Ether responds to vibration. When the tangiferous Ether responds, it imparts to the nerves a certain quiver, corresponding to that vibration. Thus we sense physical objects by touch. This is the basis of the Physical sense of touch. The sensory nerves communicate the impression to the center of Consciousness, the Organ of Observation. Thus we are conscious of the touch, conscious of it, apparently at that point where we come in physical contact with it; but remember this: You do not feel the object; you never felt an object in your life. You may take hold of anything, but you do not feel it. You feel the Etheric Emanation coming from it. You do not feel the object at all. It is that Etheric Emanation which causes your nerves of tactility to respond to it, but it must be the Tangiferous Ether, the ether of tactility else it will not produce any such impression, it will not act upon the tactile nerves, for they are keyed to the vibration of this Tangiferous Ether and can not respond to any other. This is physical touch; but it is possible for the currents of the Tangiferous Ether, passing into the Etheric Double or Magnetic Body itself, to respond without the nerves responding. When they respond, the vibration will be conveyed to Observation through this Tangiferous Ether, therefore, you will feel the object which is transmitting these etheric vibrations.

Now, you can readily understand why the Ether itself will respond to a much finer vibration than the tactile nerves will, they being grossly physical, being solid, while it is simply etheric. The result is, when the Etheric Double or Magnetic Body itself has learned to feel things independently of the nerves, you can feel many things that you could not before. Thus you are brought in contact with the Etheric Double of each object and are able to sense it. You are able to sense the Magnetic Bodies of people with whom you come in contact, and to feel them and feel what is going on there. It is in this way that psychometry enables us to diagnose patients. We feel the etheric condition and there is the real seat of disease. Before disease ever manifests itself in the gross body it has already taken place in the Magnetic Body. By sensing this etheric condition we can, therefore, take steps to remove it before it accumulates in the form of a physical condition.

We can tell the nature of the etheric principle in everyone with whom we come in contact.

Another important feature is the aid of Psychometry

in telling when things have magnetic bodies, for the one who is etherically psychometric can tell with exact certainty whether an object has a Magnetic Body or not, because he is able to respond to it and, therefore, knows this. Also it is possible to respond to all Etheric Bodies. The psychometrist can, consequently, tell all about atoms and molecules; can tell the difference between electricity and magnetism; he can tell the nature of gravitation and all those points in physics which are at the present time merely speculative philosophy; which will always be speculative to the one who has not arrived at transcendent knowledge.

But this is not all. It must be borne in mind that the ethers are not simply on the plane of physical ether. This term "Ether" is originally the "Aether" of the Latin; and exactly the same as the Sanskrit term "Akasha," which included mind, life, Astral matter and everything of the kind. It was, in fact, that energy of which all things are formed, and is very closely analogous to what is now termed force by physicists; but the physical dogmatists have at last accepted the physical aspect of Father Aether, but have made this the sole ether, having refused to accept anything higher. As a matter of fact the five Aethers or Tattvas are five manifestations of the Great Breath on all the planes of nature; therefore, Astral matter, desire stuff, has its Tangiferous Ether, which is the same as that in the physical ether. Consequently, we can in this way, come in contact with the Astral Bodies of different objects as well as people, through our sense of touch, acting in the same way through our own Desire Body, providing the Tangiferous Ether in our Desire Body is awakened sufficiently to bring us into contact with the Desire World. In this way we are able to feel the emotions of people, to feel emotions in the Desire World. We are able also, to feel the Astral Bodies of objects with which we come in contact and, therefore, able to know that they have Desire Bodies.

Again, the Mental Body has its Tangiferous Ether; therefore, by polarizing ourselves with the world without, by training our Tangiferous Ether in the Mental Body to respond to vibrations, we will be enabled to feel thought, to feel the mental impulses, to diagnose the minds of people with whom we come in contact, not by catching their thought telepathically or anything of that kind, but simply by feeling their thoughts; by the vibratory sensations which will be imparted to our Mental Body. Thus we can feel thought with our Mental Bodies, just as literally as we can feel objects of a physical nature with our physical touch. We can also come in contact with the Mental Bodies of different objects so that we will know definitely that those objects have Mental Bodies.

Likewise, the Buddhi has its Tangiferous Ether. Thus we can actually feel the soul of things when we have developed Buddhic Psychometry. We can sense them and know that they have souls, likewise, the quality and nature of those souls. Again, it is possible for us to sense the reason and the forces active upon the Buddhic plane. But this is not all. The Atma has its Tangiferous Ether, likewise, and thus we are able to sense all spiritual activities just as objectively as we do the objects of a physical character. When we have risen to this state we are able to know the spiritual world in the same way that we know the physical world, that is, so far as touch is concerned, for it is, in reality, touching the spiritual world; that is what we do; we touch it; that is, our Tangiferous Ether responds to the vibrations of the

Tangiferous Ether of the spiritual world, and, therefore, our spirit touches the spiritual world and feels those impressions.

In this way Psychometry will elevate our touch so that on whatever plane our Tangiferous Ether is operative, there we will be able to touch all those things.

Psychometry demonstrates beyond the shadow of a doubt, the septenary nature of objects. What is the logical conclusion from this? If all objects are septenary, they have experiences. They have gone through certain experiences, and if they have Mental Bodies, they are capable of learning by experience, and if so, their experiences are bound to make them think about things, and if they think, impressions will be made by their thinking, and if this be true, they must have memory. They must remember the experiences they have gone through.

If they have Desire Bodies, they are bound to go through a certain measure of emotion; they are bound to be endowed with imagination, and if so, their pleasurable and painful sensations must be stored up in their consciousness. The past experiences of objects must be known to them, must be stored up in their memories. If we could just tap this memory now and find out what these objects know, could bring ourselves into a state of union so that we could come into possession of the past experiences of the objects, we would know as much as they do; we would not have to study nature objectively any longer, but could study it subjectively. We would be able to make its experiences our own. This is just what Psychometry enables us to do. We do not have to study zoology in the objective, speculative way that the physicists do; all we have to do is take the fossil and psychometrize it and get its own experiences; it will tell us. Its memory is stored up there, so that by psychometrizing the fossil of the antediluvian world, we can actually get the memory of that fossil. We can actually know what was in the mind, in the memory of the animal at the time fossilization began, at the time of death. We can know just what it was. Therefore, it is possible by psychometrizing the fossil, to recover the history of the world zoologically and botanically, before this fossilization occurred. But not only is this true, but the septenary principle still exists in the fossil. Psychometry demonstrates that the fossil itself is still living. It is not dead; it is simply a different kind of life. Therefore, all the life experiences of the fossil as such, are stored up in it. As a consequence, it is possible to recover the entire zoological history since that began, therefore, speculative reasoning must be set aside.

We have in Psychometry the means of formulating a perfectly exact science of zoology, with speculation entirely eliminated. Not only is that true, but by taking a piece of a meteor, a piece of meteoric iron, for instance, and psychometrizing it, it is possible to discover the past experiences of that and find the planet it came from, to get its experience and thus learn its nature. Likewise by the psychometrizing of a fragment of a meteorite. Meteorological phenomena, therefore, which are beyond the reach of physical research are brought clearly within the realm of psychometric investigation.

We can in this way, learn the nature of everything. We can psychometrize a bit of rock and tell just what it is. Our study of zoology, meteorology, mineralogy, chemistry, botany and paleontology—everything of that kind, can be brought into the realm of exact science without the possibility of error. We can study botany— by psychometrizing plants, we can get in conscious touch with them so that they will tell us their life experiences, so that we will be able to measure the soul of the plants and perfectly and accurately diagnose it.

Thus, through psychometry, the entire arrangement of science may be revolutionized. For the assaying of mineral, for instance, it is impossible to make an error. Not only is that true, but the assayer, by psychometrizing a fragment of the mineral, is able to tell the size of the vein; he is able to tell whether or not the quality of the mineral improves as you go down. He can, in a word, place man in possession, of all the facts connected with a deposit of ore, simply by psychometrizing a cubic inch of it; he can tell whether or not it will pay to mine this ore. He can tell the lay of the ground and everything of that kind.

Another important feature in psychometry is the ability to diagnose one's character, life, etc., by psychometrizing an article magnetized by him. This is done by reason of the fact that everything we touch becomes charged with our Aura and our Aura vibrates in harmony with our thinking, our feeling and every activity of our being. As we magnetize an article, there is imparted to it the vibration which perfectly duplicates our own. It is, in fact, our own vibration and it stays there as long as that object exists, though, of course, it may take on other vibrations, also; consequently it is much safer to psychometrize an article that only one person has handled; but the degree to which we are able to sense the vibration proceeding from an object is wonderful. For instance, you can take a small fragment of iron, a bit of a shell from a battle field, and by psychometrizing it, you can see the perfect picture of the battle just as it is going on. How is this possible? Simply in this way: when the man picks up the shell to place it in the gun, there is in his imagination a vivid picture of the battle just as he sees is. This picture sets up in his Aura the vibration corresponding to it. The result is the shell is charged with that vibration. When it is fired it continues to retain that magnetism and vibrates in that way. When the sensitive touches it she responds to that vibration, therefore, the picture occurs in her mind. She feels this sensation. Professor Denton's wife psychometrized a bit of plaster which came from Cicero's house in Rome, she not knowing this, yet she actually described a caucus of the Roman Senators who appeared there in the house. The thought, the imagination, and everything had charged the plaster wall and had remained there ever since, consequently, we see magnetism is never exhausted. For two thousand years or thereabouts, the plaster had been charged with this magnetism, and faithfully transmitted the same. The Aura imparts whatever is in the consciousness of the person at the time, and not only that, but whatever is still in the Aura, although he may not be conscious of it —his mental state, his emotional state, his imagination, his feelings, his spiritual and soul aspirations, the nature is imparted to it, so that by psychometrizing it, you are able to take on the same condition that was present in him. That is how Psychometry is so great in soul measuring. We take on the condition of the one being diagnosed. Thus we feel just as he felt. We can diagnose his physical condition in the same way. We can tell when he is mad and when he is in a good humor. We can tell his attitude and what he intends to do, for psychometry opens the way to the feelings of the one under diagnosis by means of the article.

It is for this reason that wearing other people's clothes is so dangerous. You are likely to take on the

condition of the person. If one gets sick and dies, by
wearing the clothes of the dead person, you are likely
to contract his disease, or if you do not contract it, you
are likely to suffer the pain he suffered, and everything
of the kind. A mean man's clothes are very likely to
transmit his meanness to the one who wears them. On
the same principle, a good man sanctifies his clothing
with his own goodness, his spirituality. They become
magnetized in that way and are consequently, advantageous. It is this principle which is at the foundation
of the blessing of different articles.

The house also can be sensed. We can take on the
condition of every house we enter, of the building, and
thus diagnose its character, its influence; and the
"creepy" feeling that you get in going into certain
houses, is due to psychometry. You are taking on the
psychometric condition of the place, thus, you have this
creepy sensation.

There is, in fact, no field of research which can not
be entered through psychometry, for it is simply the
sense of touch capable of infinite elevation and extension. It is capable of being extended to every part of the
universe. The more sensitive you are in your feelings,
the more you are able to come in contact with. The psychometrist while lecturing can literally hold his hand on
the pulse of his audience and tell how much it can stand.
He may, at the same time, sense that there is some one
in the audience who needs certain things; thus a public
lecture may develop into a heart to heart talk to a certain individual in the audience because the lecturer
senses his demand. You can adjust your mind to the
audience.

In going down the street you can feel the spirit of the
crowd. You can tell just what it is. You can look into

the very hearts of men, psychometrically. You can know, absolutely, humanity. The statement that we have to judge by appearances; that we cannot look into the hearts of people, is not true, for the psychometrist, unfortunately, not only can, but can not help himself; that is the difficulty. You not only can look into the hearts of people, but you cannot help yourself; you take on the condition of people when it would sometimes be much more agreeable if you were a little gross, so that you did not sense their conditions.

And so this touch brings us into that perfect contact with nature so that we can know; we can be in possession of first hand knowledge, through touch. This is only one of the psychical senses, but it will do this.

Remember, therefore, psychometry is not an unmixed blessing. It is an excellent thing for the scientist, for the one engaged in research because he can know truth that cannot be ascertained otherwise, but, remember, it has its inconveniences. It is not at all nice when you call on some friends and they tell you how delighted they are to see you, how sweet it is for you to come, and you know every moment they are lying; that they wish you were at the botton of the lake; you know all the time they are wanting you to leave. It is not so very comfortable always when you get up to deliver a lecture and you feel the magnetism, the wish for you to shut up. Even if they do not say it, you know it is in their hearts. It is not agreeable. You know flattery is pleasant; it is nice. We like to receive it, but we do not like to know while we are receiving it, that it is flattery, and the trouble with the psychometrist is, he always knows it is flattery.

Another important aid in psychometry is the ability to take a letter and psychometrize it while reading it.

In this way you can read between the lines and tell what the person was thinking of while he was writing. He writes, perhaps, lies, on the face of the paper, but he writes the truth in the paper. When you learn to sense that vibration, you know what he was thinking and then you can never be deceived by a letter. When you learn to psychometrize you will always know it is deceitful; know just what was in the person's mind.

Another thing: by psychometry you can shake hands with a person and right at the time you are shaking hands you can psychometrize him and tell just what is in his mind and know just what you have to deal with.

Thus it is all the way along. At the same time, it is disagreeable.

What, then, are we to do to prevent this disagreeable psychometrizing? Remain positive; but remember, you cannot psychometrize while positive. You can keep from sensing the people; but you must take on the condition of the people if you get anything; but by being positive, forming a shell around you, you can shut yourself off, to a great extent.

Some of you may want to know how it is to be developed. By becoming more sensitive. Psychometry is a sensitive condition of the Tangiferous Ether. By remaining sensitive and trying to feel things. Open yourself; become negative and take on the condition of everything with which you come in contact. Diagnose patients psychometrically; psychometrize articles; it will all tend to make the form more sensitive. At the same time, revise your thinking and reason. Become more subtile, more sensitive in all the activities of your life. At the same time, let your physical life be such as will sensitize the physical ether, and that can be done only by first leading a celibate life, or if not a celibate life, at least a continent life. The nearer you come to celibacy, the better conserved the sex energy, the more lust is overcome, and everything of that kind, the more the system can be refined and more highly organized.

Then, the next important point is the diet. No person will succeed as a psychometrist for any practical purpose, who lives on a meat diet. The finer the diet is, the better, and a diet exclusively of fruit is much better than anything else, and the nearer you come to that, the better.

Again, one should not over eat. No one who is corpulent can ever be an expert psychometrist. The body must be fine, not heavy. In fact, emaciation assists this psychometric sense a great deal. Fasting is of advantage in this way.

Also live alone as much as possible. Keep away from the world. Avoid sensations as much as possible, so that you will not become entangled by coming in contact with them. In fact, the greatest seers live almost entirely alone, and the custom of the ancients in having the oracles absolutely separated from all contact with the world, so that they never saw people until they came to get a response, was quite wise, quite expedient.

In a word, the power to psychometrize is in proportion to the degree of sensitivity in the Aura, and this must be obtained by common sense methods, and, remember, general development is no advantage, so far as conferring psychometry is concerned. This is through the development of the Tangiferous Ether alone. If some other ether is developed, some other sense will present itself. It is for this reason that it is not so advantageous to try to secure these senses, these powers, because by so doing you switch the current of your development in this particular direction and prevent the higher development.

LESSON XI

CLAIROLFACTIOUSNESS

Clairolfactiousness is the psychical sense of smell, corresponding to smelling exactly as Clairvoyance does to seeing, Clairaudience to hearing, and Psychometry to touch. It is usually the fourth sense to be developed, following immediately after Psychometry.

All objects have their Odoriferous Ether the same as the others. By reason of this odoriferous ether there is a vibration expressing itself in odor which is present in the Aura on all the planes, through all the principles present in that Aura. Each rate of vibration expressing itself through the five Tattvas, produces a corresponding odor, by reason of the vibration in the Odoriferous Ether. This odor does not produce any sound, any light or anything of that kind although it is the odoriferous manifestation of the same vibration which produces light in the Luminiferous Ether, and sound in the Sonoriferous Ether. The ether of space, together with the higher principles, acts as the plastic medium between the different Auras. Thus the Odoriferous Ether of space becomes the connecting link between the Odoriferous Ether in one Aura and that of another, enabling a continuous flow of the vibrations to pass from that Aura to the Aura of another body. It is in this way that the Odoriferous Ether in any object communicates with that in man. Thus he is enabled to sense the odor of any object, and all smelling is produced in this way. Odoriferous vibration awakens a vibratory response in the Olfactory nerve which thus communicates the vibration to the Organ of Observation and through the nerve center of smell, enabling us to sense the odor. When the vibratory response comes through the Olfactory nerve, we become acquainted with this object through our sense of smell, not through some other; that is the impression we get of it; the sensation we receive from it is one of odor, pleasant if it be in harmony with our general vibration, unpleasant if it be otherwise.

It should also be borne in mind that the different rates of vibration express themselves in different odors. We get an impression of a certain vibration by a certain odor. This will be readily understood if we realize that that odor in the first place was the result of this same rate of vibration. We sense an odor simply because the rate of vibration which expressed itself in that odor is reproduced in our own Odoriferous Ether.

Ordinary smelling is the sensation of Odoriferous vibration through the Olfactory nerve, but the Olfactory nerve, being physical, is unable to respond to anything higher than gross physical vibration. It cannot bring us into the cognition of the higher etheric or any of the higher principles. Why is it that we smell flowers as we approach them? How does the odor of a flower garden reach us when we are a long distance from it? Simply by means of the Odoriferous ether in the atmosphere, the Odoriferous Ether in the flower acting upon that, thus transmitting the vibration to us, when the same vibration being awakened in our Odoriferous Ether, through our Olfactory nerve, we thus become conscious of the influence; but it should be borne in mind that the ordinary person can smell only those odors, the vibration of which is sufficiently powerful to move his olfactory nerve, when that nerve is able to respond to them. Whenever the vibration is higher than the ability for a gross physical response, we are unable to sense the odor.

Thus it will be seen that the ordinary person does not smell the finer odors, not because they do not exist, but because his olfactory nerve will not respond to the vibratory impulse and he has not as yet developed any other channel for such response. When the Odoriferous Ether in the Magnetic Body has been so developed as to respond to vibratory impulses operative in the ether in the world without, he will begin to smell independently of the olfactory nerve, this Ether being the channel between his own consciousness and the world without. He will, in this way, sense Odoriferous vibrations of too high an order to create any impression upon the olfactory nerve. Thus the odors present in the finer ether are made possible. He can sense the odors of the Magnetic Bodies of different people and will thus be able to diagnose disease by the odor of persons, to tell the specific diseases; also to recognize the state of health, and recognize the difference between a magnetic and an electrical person, a positive and a negative one, by reason of their Odoriferous emanations. Further, he will be able to sense atoms, molecules and everything of that kind, in fact, everything of an etheric character. Also, he will be able to smell different minerals by reason of their etheric emanations, to tell one metal from another. In the same way he will become an expert at smelling out deposits of ore and everything of that kind, in the most literal sense of the word.

It is difficult for the ordinary person to realize the degree to which this sense of smell may be developed. A Hottentot in South Africa is able to smell water at a distance of a quarter of a mile, by sniffing the air. In other words, his sense of smell is so acute that he can tell the difference between dry air and moist air, by the odor. Again, the blacks of Australia are as good as any bloodhound at tracing out, running down criminals.

When the Odoriferous Ether in the Desire Body has been awakened and trained to respond, it will be found that everything pertaining to the Desire Planes will be brought within the range of our sense of smell. It must, in fact, be understood that the moment the Odoriferous Ether of the Desire Body begins to operate, everything in the Desire World will be brought to our cognition, for it must be borne in mind that there are seven notes on the Desire octave and these notes correspond to the seven sub-planes in this Desire world. The result is, one may be able to sense those things on one note, but not another. The range of development in the Odoriferous Ether in your Desire Body must determine the range of its activity in the Desire world, but, subject to this limitation, we will be able to smell other Desire Bodies, thus to diagnose their character, to realize their emotions, their feelings; not only see into, but literally smell out the hearts of men and to tell the character of any emotion by the odor we receive.

The Clairolfactious sensitive can, consequently, tell just the attitude an audience bears to him while he is speaking, by reason of the odors he senses from time to time. Likewise he can tell the kind of people he is coming amongst by the odors he senses.

As the sensitive develops to the Mental Plane and there awakens his Odoriferous Ether, his Mental Body is polarized with the Mental Plane and thus he can smell thoughts, mental bodies, forces in the mental world and everything of that kind; and when his Causal body is awakened, the same thing in the region of abstract thought.

When the Odoriferous Ether of his Buddhic Body is developed so that it will respond to vibration in the

Odoriferous Ether without, he is able to smell all the forces of the Buddhic Plane, the Buddhic bodies of people—to smell the souls of men. In other words, to attain the realization of truth, quite as effectively as he can by seership, by hearing or by feeling. When his Spiritual Odoriferous Ether is developed and he is able to respond to that of the spiritual world, he will be able to sense all activities and forces in that world, to smell the spirits and thus tell the character of any one spirit by reason of the odor he receives. Now, the odor of sanctity that was so much praised in the hagiology of the mediæval church and which has been so terribly criticised by the fool rationalists ever since, is founded upon a realization of this odor. It is the odor which emanates from one because of the sanctity of his or her life; it is the odor produced by the spiritual activities of a given individual; the individual is spiritual, is living on a high spiritual plane and because of his spiritual character, his meditation, his high development, he reaches a certain rate of vibration which is not reached by the ordinary person. Because of this rate of vibration, certain odors are emanated from him and when another one's Odoriferous Ether is able to respond to this vibration he will sense that odor. The result is the odor of sanctity is sensed in proportion to one's spirituality, just as it is transmitted in proportion to one's spirituality. When one develops his own spirit in connection with the spirit of God, is a mystic, in other words, there is emanated an odor, not properly pertaining to the human spirit in any sense whatever—an odor which can go out only from a spirit in conjunction with God's spirit. Such an odor can be sensed only by one in the same attitude, by one who is likewise living in conjunction with the Spirit of God. Not only, however, is it true that there is an odor of sanctity, but it is also true that the practitioner of Black Magic, of the dark art, emanates a devilish odor. The stories about the brimstone breath of the warlocks are not at all fictitious, for the one who deals with Satan, the one who has developed a Satanic character, actually emanates a stench corresponding to his character, which stench can be sensed by the sensitive who has the Odoriferous Ether sufficiently developed, and thus can be avoided, for he can always be recognized.

Now, the stories about having persons employed for the purpose of smelling out witches, illustrate a great truth. It is possible for one who has this sense sufficiently developed and who knows how to recognize the odor of a satanic character, to smell out witches every time, without fail; but, of course, it would be highly necessary that he be one who had this developed to the highest point of seership, otherwise there would be great danger of the innocent suffering for the guilty.

Remember, there is nothing in all the universe that does not emanate an odor peculiar to itself. By this odor the nature of the object may be sensed.

Likewise every statement, every truth, every fact has an odor which will express its character, which will enable the sensitive to identify it. One who is a Clairolfactorist may employ his power in conjunction with psychometry; that is, he can hold an article in his hand, psychometrize it, and if he be a clairolfactorist at the same time he will get the odor corresponding to its nature. He will be psychometrizing through his sense of smell, and he may not be able to get the impression otherwise at all. He may not be able to do true psychometrizing, but at the same time he will receive the odor and thus can depend upon it.

Clairolfactiousness is developed in the same general

way that the other senses are. The principle of your
Aura must be generally sensitized. This, of course, is
accomplished in the same way that the sensitizing is
carried on for the other activities; by refining the emotions, the thinking, the reasoning, intuition and everything of that kind; by leading the most spiritual life
possible, at the same time refining the diet, purifying
the body by living a life of celibacy and all of those
things.

The specific Ether, the Odoriferous, is refined and developed by exercising the sense of smell as much as possible; by always trying to sense the difference in odors;
by trying to distinguish between as many different kinds
of odors as possible; and anything that interferes with
the smell should be removed, eliminated.

A very good Yoga practice for such development is
to sit in the silence a few minutes every day and concentrate the attention on the tip of the nose. This may
sound ridiculous; nevertheless, if you will try it, say
for fifteen minutes twice every day, sitting and contem-
plating the end of your nose, centering all your attention
there, in two or three weeks you will begin to smell odors
that you could not smell any other time, and you will,
in the course of time, accomplish most satisfactory results, but you can exercise your sense of smell through
any given vehicle of consciousness, only in proportion
as that vehicle is developed. Your Odoriferous Ether
itself may be highly developed, but the principle in which
you are functioning may be very low. You must, therefore, develop the general human constitution and make
the development of the Odoriferous Ether secondary to
that. But if the development is carried on properly, that
is, the Odoriferous Ether developed in conjunction with
the different principles of the Aura, you will find you

will be able to exercise your sense of smell quite satisfactorily and by such exercises you will reach a much broader range of perception than at the present time seems possible.

The sense of smell is itself precisely the same as Clairolfactiousness, the only difference being that the former is through the olfactory nerve, while the latter is through the Odoriferous Ether in some principle of the Aura, direct. Thus by developing that ether in any one or more of the principles of the Aura we will have Clairolfactious smelling just as simple, as natural as we have the ordinary physical sense of smell, being just as much so as the physical is, nothing metaphysical, nothing mysterious, but being simply an extension of the ordinary sense of smell along the same lines as it manifests in the physical sense, but through the diverse principles in the Aura. It is, therefore, not another sense, but merely the physical sense of smell almost infinitely magnified and extended. It is CLEAR SMELLING, in other words, instead of smelling greatly obscured and limited.

LESSON XII

CLAIRGUSTIENCE

Clairgustience is the metaphysical sense of taste, bearing the same relation to ordinary taste that Clairolfactiousness does to the ordinary olfactory sense. It is merely an extension of the sense of taste into the physical realm. It is not to be understood as a spiritual sense, separate and apart from the physical sense of taste, but is that sense of taste extended into the realm of the psychical—in fact, manifesting on all the planes of nature.

In order to understand the working of this sense it is necessary that we should first understand the rationale of physical taste.

How do we taste? What is the basis of the sense of taste? All objects have a Gustiferous ether as well as the other four ethers. This Gustiferous ether corresponds to hydrogen when it descends to the gaseous state, and is, consequently the negative-electric principle. All Auras are charged with this Gustiferous ether and present this principle in their activities at any and all times. That is to say, whenever the Aura is present the five ethers are active at the same time, the result being, of course, the activity of the Gustiferous ether along with the others. The activity of the Aura, of course, manifests in and through vibration. This vibration corresponds to the nature of the activity going on in the Aura. This vibration expresses itself in all the five Tattvas, resulting in the transmission of Gustatory vibration, the same as the other Tattvic vibration.

As the Aura vibrates upon the surrounding ether, it causes the Gustiferous ether of space to act as the plastic medium between its Gustiferous ether and that of any other Aura that may receive its vibrations. The Gustiferous ether of space is now the plastic medium, uniting the Gustiferous ether of the vibrating Aura and that of all other Auras by becoming the sensitizing element between the two. Thus the vibratory quiver is communicated from one Aura to another. This vibration, coming in contact with our Aura imparts to the gustatory nerve a quiver corresponding to the vibration in the object from which the Auric sensation proceeds, thus communicating to our sense of taste the same rate of vibration.

Ordinarily speaking, this sense of taste comes only when we bring objects into close contact with the gustatory nerve, in the act of mastication, or where it relates to liquids, swallowing, etc. The taste buds on the tongue are merely the ends of the branching nerves and nerve filaments that reach out and take notice of the different gustatory emanations; they are able to respond to those vibrations and are, in fact, attuned to various kinds of vibrations, so that some of them will taste one rate of vibration and some another. Almost every imaginable flavor may be responded to in this way. As food is being masticated, this emanation is continually passing from it, striking the taste buds, which respond to the vibration and are thus carried along the gustatory nerve to the center of taste located on the fourth ventricle, which is in communication with the Faculty of Observation, thus producing a thought which corresponds to the nature of the object. The identification of the object is made in this way, through its taste. When we have identified the object, we telegraph, as it were, to the stomach, notifying it of the kind of food we have taken into the mouth, and it pours forth a form of gastric juice suited to the purpose of digestion. Likewise, when it is a food that must be digested in the mouth, the saliva is specially prepared for the digestion of this kind of food.

It follows that the main feature in digestion is the appreciation of the food, which we secure from our faculty of taste. It is mainly in the recognition of the food, its identification while mastication is going on. This is all expressed through the gustatory nerve, whenever anything is taken into the mouth, whenever it is brought into close proximity to the gustatory nerve. But it will readily be realized that the field of gustation open to the gustatory nerve is comparatively small, owing to its rigidity, its inability to respond to the higher rates of vibration, consequently all gustation above the range of physical response or below the range of such response will be absolutely imperceptible to one who has not developed some of the higher phases of this gustatory sense. But it must be remembered that physical taste is merely the response of the gustatory nerve to etheric vibration. It is the vibration of the Gustiferous ether striking against the gustatory nerve and causing it to move, that produces the beginning of the gustatory sense at any one time. Therefore, if we can teach the Etheric Double to respond, it will follow that we shall have the same system of taste extended over a much broader field than would be possible in the ordinary way of tasting.

The Magnetic Body contains its Gustiferous ether, the same as every other body, and when this Gustiferous ether has learned to respond to the vibrations in the Gustiferous ether in whatever it comes in contact with,

it will communicate the response to the center of consciousness and thus we will taste without the agency
of the gustatory nerve. Not only is this true, but we do
not have to take anything in the mouth in order to taste
it, but may hold it in the hand or bring it about the
body, just so as to bring its Gustiferous ether into
conjunction with our own, so that the emanation may
reach our center of consciousness.

Again we can taste anything having an etheric emanation. Different minerals and chemicals may be recognized in this way.

Likewise, different diseases can be recognized by the
taste of them. A healthy person can be recognized almost
instantly by the taste which comes to one as a result
of being in his vicinity. Medicines may be easily recognized. It can be told quite readily when one is being
poisoned, by tasting the poison in his system, by reason
of the gustative emanations coming from his Magnetic
Body.

Also we can tell the strength of the electrical and
magnetic currents, in fact everything of an etheric character, either in the Aura or in the space around us—
anywhere in fact. The entire etheric range is brought
into our consciousness through the taste, which is not
that of the gross body, but of the magnetic body, acting
through the center of consciousness, the same as the
ordinary taste.

Likewise when the Gustiferous Ether of the Desire
Body has been trained to respond to vibration we will
be enabled to taste everything on the Desire Plane. All
emotional states may be tasted quite readily. We can
taste spirits at seances and thus recognize their character. We can taste the Desire Bodies of people and thus
tell whether or not we want anything to do with them,

and in these higher forms of Clairgustience, it is not
necessary that the object be brought into physical contact with us, but we can taste anything whenever its
Astral principle is brought into communication with our
own Astral or Desire principle. It is in this way that we
are able to recognize all those forces on the Desire plane
without coming into physical contact with them.

Further, as we develop the Gustiferous Ether in our
Mental and Causal Bodies, we become able to recognize
thought and all the activities of the Mental Plane, in-
cluding the qualities of different mental bodies, through
the emanations which reach us from them. Thus our
Gustiferous Mental Ether responds to whatever vibration comes to it; thus the quality of that vibration is
recognized through the sensation of taste which it produces.

On the Buddhic and Spiritual planes also Clairgustience is possible by reason of the Gustiferous Ether
that is operative in the Buddhi and the Atma. By reason of this Gustiferous Ether, we are able, when it is
trained and developed, to respond to vibrations of the
same principle without, and, as a result, become conscious in a gustatory manner, of the qualities operative
on those planes.

Thus, the range of gustatory sensation is quite as
great as that of seeing, hearing, smelling or feeling.

Because of the existence of the Gustiferous Ether,
we are able to respond to and thus become conscious of
the gustatory quality in all things in exact proportion
as we have developed and sensitized our Gustiferous
Ether, and no further.

All the qualities in the universe manifest a gustatory
manner quite as much as in any other. There is no
limit to the degree of gustatory manifestation, the limit

being in our ability to sense the same. We sense this
gustatory vibration in proportion to the sensitivity of
our Gustiferous Ether, consequently as is the development of one's Gustiferous Ether so will be his Gustiferous perception.

When we have developed this sense we come to realize
the truth that all things have a Gustiferous Ether; that
it is this which is the foundation of all taste and that it
is not necessary for one to come in physical contact with
an object in order to taste it. This can be verified quite
easily by one who has developed the first stages of Clairgustience. It is quite easy for such a person to walk
through an orchard and taste the peaches growing on
the trees. This is not stated in reference to one's tasting
simply by reason of focusing the thought on the taste of
the fruit, but is used with reference to cases where one
does not know intellectually, how the fruit tastes. It
is a clear case of gustatory perception, without coming
within ten feet of the tree on which the fruit is growing.
Fruit may be brought into a room on a dish and if it be
fresh, that is, living fruit, it is quite possible for one
with a slight degree of etheric Clairgustience to taste it
before it reaches the table. There are thousands of other
instances that might be cited, demonstrative of the great
truth that all living things, vegetables as well as animals,
have their Gustiferous Ether and consequently, their
Magnetic Bodies.

Now, when on the Astral Plane there comes to one the
same gustatory sensation that he receives while tasting
fruit either physically or etherically; then he knows that
he is tasting Astral emanations of the fruit or whatever
it may be, consequently he knows that there is an Astral
existence for those things; and as we go on to the different planes, we know that there is really a Mental, a

Buddhic and a Spiritual principle appertaining to every object in existence, and the statements made from time to time as to spirits enjoying certain kinds of food, enjoying the emanations from the food, are found to be in perfect harmony with the scientific knowledge which we have secured in the investigation of nature, Clairgustatively.

Clairgustience is "Clear Tasting;" that is, the etheric taste without any of the marring influences of those limitations which are ordinarily put upon the forces of nature, by reason of the forms which usually veil them.

We can understand how it is that the brain will respond to these higher vibrations to which the nerves will not respond, when we realize that there is in each principle an exact duplicate of the faculties; that the gross physical brain corresponds to the gross physical body and is merely the channel through which these finer principles function. Consequently there is an Astral and a Mental, a Magnetic and a Buddhic, as well as an Atmic brain; consequently those responses are made by those principles, the same as the gross physical brain responds to the gross physical vibration.

In order to develop Clairgustience, it is well to sit a few moments at different times each day, with the attention fixed upon the end of the tongue and, in fact, for some little distance back, imagining, at the same time, the most delicious flavors, the most luscious gustatory sensation, and as we are thus enjoying those fine flavors, those rich gustatory sensations which we have conjured up by our imagination, we will, in time, reach the point where we will really enjoy them; we will really taste them. This should come on in from two to three weeks. If persisted in for a few months it will be found that we will be able to enjoy unearthly sensations. We will be able to taste things not of the earth, but the heavenly Nectar and Ambrosia are as nothing compared to what can be tasted in time.

Also you will not only taste the Nectar and Ambrosia of the Olympians, but with this will be developed a capacity for tasting flavors of a much more undesirable quality, for it is merely an extension of one's capacity for tasting all things, the unpleasant quite as easily as the pleasant, and as this is developed, we will develop a capacity for absolute, omnipotent accuracy so far as delineating the nature of things when we come in contact with them, an appreciation of the qualities manifesting, which will never deceive. This appreciation will extend not only to physical matters, but to the spiritual and all the intermediate principles, and will enable us to not only look into the hearts of men, but to taste their hearts and know, Gustatorily, what is there.

LESSON XIII

CLAIRO-DYNAMICS

The sense of Clairo-Dynamics gives to man the ability to weight metaphysical substances in the same way that the dynamic sense enables him to weigh physical substances. You will remember, the dynamic sense registers the weight of objects by reason of the percentage of muscular contraction necessary to lift them, this being the foundation of weight in a physical way. When we lift an object what we do is really to take hold of it, and the muscles contracting, thus becoming shortened, draw the bones into position so that the arms act as levers and raise the object. It is thus not a motion of the hand or arm, but a drawing of the arm by means of muscular contraction in obedience to a mental impulse transmitted through the motor nerves. The motor nerves transmit the impulse of a force which causes the contraction of the muscles, this muscular contraction resulting in the movement which lifts the object.

It was shown in the lesson on Dynamics that this is the origin of weight, that is of our sense of objects as heavy and light, the weight of any object consisting in the amount of muscular contraction necessary to raise it. We, therefore, have consciousness of weight only because of the amount of contraction which the object will cause. As we become conscious of this weight, we transmit to the faculty of weight in our minds, through the Organ of weight in the brain, an impression of this object as heavy and of the amount of contraction necessary to lift it; in other words, we register in that organ

(120)

our impression of the muscular contraction necessary to lift the object. The purpose of this faculty being, among other things, to record our impressions of weight, and weight consisting in the amount of muscular contraction necessary to overcome the gravity of the object, our faculty records that amount of contraction.

The simplest form of the dynamic sense is, therefore, the ability to pick up an object, a weight, for instance, in the hand, and guess at its weight. The weighing of objects in the hand is not merely guess work; it is the most accurate system of weighing in the world, scales being a mechanical device intended to take the place of this weighing. We will, therefore, see that by holding objects in our hands, weighing them in the hand, we will form an impression of their weight. This impression will be communicated to the faculty of weight, indicating the amount of heaviness or weight in the object. The next time an object is taken up, the impression will indicate its weight, and we will contrast it with the first impression of weight, as being heavier or lighter; as taking more contraction or not so much.

Now, the only reason why we cannot guess the weight of anything by weighing it in the hand, is because our standard of weight is different from the one used in the ordinary mechanical process of weighing. We have an artificial standard, represented in pounds, ounces, pennyweights, grains, etc., which we have built up by the use of weights; but our internal dynamic sense takes cognizance of everything from the standpoint of percentage of muscular contraction necessary to lift it. The standard of weight is, therefore, different. The difficulty is to adjust ourselves to the conventional standard. This can be done only by practice; that is, we must weigh in our hands, objects, the weight of which we know, and by associating the impression, the sensation of muscular contraction we receive, with so many pounds or ounces, we will thus translate our standard of weight into the conventional standard. The result will be whenever we have a sensation of weight, we will subconsciously translate that into the corresponding weight according to the physical scale. As a result, we will be able to guess the weight of any object by weighing it in the hand. This was shown in the lesson on Dynamics. It was also shown that the muscles would respond to any muscular contraction in the body of another person, when our muscles were in contact with his; by holding him by the hand, for instance, we would be able to sense the degree of his muscular contraction. Thus we would be able to weigh the impulses which were operative in his muscular system, and as these muscular contractions and relaxations are due to nervous stimuli and these nervous stimuli, in turn, to to mental and emotional conditions, we should learn to estimate the force of those impulses and their identity as well by means of the force they exercised upon his muscular system.

The trained muscle reader who poses as a mind reader, gives an illustration of this, and this sense explains, also, the handwritng through the muscular contraction and relaxation and the muscular movement which gives that particular tremor to the pen, which will cause the formation of the letters.

The foundation of the dynamic sense is, therefore, the ability of the muscles to respond to weight, and anything which will impart an impulse of contraction or relaxation to them and the communication of the sensation of this contraction or relaxation to the center of weight; thus a consciousness of objects as being heavy or light, will be communicated. But Clairo-dynamics goes much further, for the faculty of weight is capable of responding to impulses which would not cause a motion in the muscles; that is to say, something may have a tendency to cause a relaxation of the muscle or a contraction, but without having sufficient force to act upon it. Perhaps it is not a gross material force, but belongs to some other department of nature, in which case it will communicate the impulse to the center of weight, creating an impression there, but as this organ of weight usually deals with muscular contraction or relaxation, it will feel this impulse as a muscular movement. In other words, muscular motions will be translated into the terms of the physical. We will sense them as being physical although they are in their nature metaphysical.

It must be borne in mind also that the faculty has its center in the Organ, the Faculty being merely that part of the Mental Body which is functioning through this Organ, having its center there and which is related to those rates of vibration. It, therefore, is that part which senses the physical impulses, but will also sense mental impulses. Anything, therefore, which requires a measure of force to move it, anything which has the same relation to mind that a weight would have to muscles, will create in the mind a sensation exactly corresponding to the one resulting from the muscular displacement caused by the lifting of a weight.

All activities, on all the planes of nature, but particularly the etheric part of the physical, or Astral and the Mental, can be weighed by the Faculty of Weight. Thus we are able to estimate their comparative force. This does not give us the ability to ascertain the value of the different forces, to estimate their relative character; it enables us only to ascertain their comparative strength, their dynamic value, in other words. When we have this dynamic sensation we can just as accurately weigh thought or emotion or magnetic currents as the ordinary person can weigh physical objects.

Now, no system of weight will enable one to tell the difference between sugar and starch; that must be told by chemical test or by their appearance—by various tests, but we do tell the quantity; likewise, by this Clairo-dynamic sense, we are able to tell the strength of any force with which we come in contact; we are able to measure it quantitatively, though not qualitatively. This, being a faculty of the mind, does not take cognizance of the transcendental region; that is, Buddhi and Manas are not observed by this faculty, but everything on the Mental Plane and the Desire Plane as well, likewise all the magnetic and electric forces in the etheric region of the physical plane communicate their impressions to it, and are, in this way, measured.

The sensitive who very often feels an oppressive sensations as though she were being crushed down, as though there were a great weight crushing her down, pressing the life out of her, breaking her to pieces, is experiencing Clairo - dynamic sensation. She is taking notice of the pressure or weight of those psychical forces. Now, as a matter of fact, those forces are pressing that way on every one; perhaps not quite so much as on a sensitive, because a sensitive is usually negative to all such things, nevertheless, those forces are bearing in on every one only no one but a clairo-dynamic sensitive feels them. No one else has a faculty of weight sufficiently sensitive to register this pressure. The pressure, of course, seems to be physical because the Faculty of weight is used to register physical dynamics.

When pressure seems to act on the brain; when one feels as though there were a weight crushing the brain, he is feeling the influence of mental currents, of thought and forces in the Mental Plane, which are coming in on him. He is, as it were, a point of attraction, a nucleus around which the forces of the Mental Plane are gathering. One in this state is likely to be not an original thinker, but one who is acting as the mental channel for other forces. These may be mental Karma left by other thinkers in the past; they may be the thinking mind of some one at the present time; they may be the influence of other entities. It may be there is some Master in the world who is directing his mind and forcing him along certain lines, or it may be he is drawing on the forces of the mental Plane, the Kosmic Manas itself. In any case it comes in this way: the mental force from without is pressing in on the individual's mental body. The brain, being the center of the activity of this Body, its greatest impression is there and he senses it in this way. The fact that he senses this weight, this pressure on the brain is no evidence that the pressure is there, any more than if he did not sense it; it is merely evidence that he is becoming clairo-dynamic; that he is sensing the impact of those mental forces. Of course, it indicates that the forces are there, but the forces may be there when he does not sense them. It must, however, be very carefully observed in order to tell that this is just what it is, because in the process of thinking, the Mental Body presses outward, as it were, there is an impulse coming out to the surface. The brain is thus made to press against the cranium. There will result a sensation very closely analogous to pressure from without. It is consequently, difficult to tell whether it is your brain expanding, or a force coming from without, but in time you will be able to distinguish between the two sensations. If it be an expanding sensation, a sensation of your brain expanding, and meeting with resistance, that is an inert resistance, it will follow that it is due to your own thinking; but if you are almost inert, if you are inertly resisting, that is, passively resisting a positive impulse from without, a positive force, it will then indicate the clairo-dynamic sense. Now, one may experience this while psychometrizing an article. If so, it will be indicative of the fact that he has come in contact, through the instrumentality of this article, with a force that is acting upon him in this dynamic way.

There is nothing in the three worlds but what is able to create a dynamic impression upon the Center of Weight, the dynamic faculty of the mind, which may be sensed, providing that faculty of the mind is sufficiently sensitive and is developed. The development of one's Faculty of Weight, therefore, gives him the dynamic sense on that particular plane. This, however, does not mean that a powerful development of dynamics will give the Clairo-dynamic sense on the Astral or Mental Plane. This can follow only when there is a powerful development of Weight in conjunction with the awakening and development of the Desire Body or the Mental Body as the case may be. The Causal Body would have to be developed in conjunction with Weight, to enable one to measure the dynamic value of abstract thought and abstract mental impulses, also the impression of mental and causal bodies, as well as desire Bodies by reason of the sensation of weight which we experience by coming in contact with them, is to be estimated according to this faculty.

Clairo-dynamics is not something separate and distinct; there is not a sharp line between it and physical dynamics; it is merely an extension of the dynamic sense, into the metaphysical region. However, it is to be distinguished from physical dynamics in this way; in physical dynamics the sensation is communicated to the dynamic center through the muscles, but in Clairo-Dynamics it is communicated through the Magnetic Body or Desire Body, or the Mental Body or the Causal Body, independently of the physical body; also it is communicated to the mental faculty independently of its physical organ.

CPSIA information can be obtained
at www.ICGtesting.com
Printed in the USA
BVHW010944091020
590692BV00012B/205